2007

2008

THE BRYAN SERIES

Guilford COLLEGE

Creating Community Conversation Since 1996

In 1837, the Religious Society of Friends (Quakers) founded the New Garden Boarding School to prepare women and men for a lifetime of learning, work, and constructive action dedicated to the betterment of the world. Now known as Guilford College, the institution has a commitment to a transformative liberal arts education for all students with an emphasis on principled problem-solving. The college maintains core values of community, diversity, equality, excellence, integrity, justice and stewardship.

Since 1996, Guilford has created community conversation by presenting national and international leaders, renowned authors and other esteemed individuals in the Bryan Series. Previous speakers have included Desmond Tutu, Mikhail Gorbachev, Colin Powell, Sidney Poitier, Madeleine Albright, Ken Burns, Bill Moyers, Mary Robinson, David McCullough and Toni Morrison.

This year, Guilford welcomes six more distinguished speakers. The community conversation begins in September, with three award-winning actors in a one-night event, and continues with internationally best-selling author Isabel Allende in November, former U.S. Representative J.C. Watts in February and Pulitzer Prize-winning journalist Bob Woodward in April.

www.guilford.edu/bryanseries

Excellence

Diversity

Equality

Community

Integrity

Stewardship

Justice

Ask Charlie

Ask Charlie

THE LIFE AND TIMES OF GUILFORD COLLEGE LEGEND
CHARLES C. HENDRICKS

By
Robin McWilliams

CHAPEL HILL
PRESS, INC.®

ISBN Number 1-880849-58-5
Library of Congress Catalog Number 2003103484
Printed in the United States of America
07 06 05 04 03   10 9 8 7 6 5 4 3 2 1

THESE WORDS ARE DEDICATED IN MEMORY OF:

Richard Hendricks...
brother, roommate,
and best friend.

Virginia Lane Pleasants...
'star rester,' faithful
and eternal friend.

CONTENTS

FOREWORD

I came up to Guilford College in the fall of 1949 from the crossroads town of Biscoe only fifty miles away. It was a giant leap, however, for a kid from a town that small and from a family that had everything except money. I told Charlie that I needed help and he put me to work in the dining hall. My first impression of him was that he had unflagging energy. He worked all of the time. Up early, he managed the dining hall for three meals a day, ran the soda shop at night while looking after the bookstore as well. I never saw him when I thought he was tired but I don't believe he was ever able to get to bed (he lived in Archdale Hall at the time) before midnight.

In addition to his official duties, he always had time to be a true friend to the students. I never asked a favor of him that was denied. He drove an old car then, a Chevrolet. There were probably less than a dozen students who had cars on campus at that time. If Charlie wasn't using his car, more than likely he had given a student permission to borrow it. His generosity has always been phenomenal and his heart as big as the sea. I recall times when I borrowed the car and then asked Charlie to lend me some money to put gas in it.

Charlie moved quickly in everything he did. He talked fast, walked fast, his hands moved quickly to a task… and as I think back on it, I realize with that kind of work overload that he had to act quickly. He did not once complain and became, over the years, the most valued member of the college staff. He was, and continues to be, the greatest mentor in school history. He got to know our parents, our girlfriends, and we confided in him. He was aware of, and sympathetic with, our struggles with finances, grades, and girls.

His memory is astounding. He remembers thousands of us! I recently set this scenario for him: "If all of us who attended Guilford from the mid-forties to the mid-fifties were standing out in a great field, could you not walk among us and come up with every single name?" He paused, tears filled his eyes, and he replied that he probably could.

Charlie's loyalty to the college is legend. He never was asked to do anything that he did not accept with wholehearted commitment and enthusiasm. His work in recruiting, fundraising, and public relations has been a great part of Guilford's success in becoming one of the best small colleges in the nation. He is the go-to guy when something needs to be done.

Simply put… Charlie Hendricks is Guilford College just as much as Winston Churchill is England and Michael Jordan is basketball. His love for the college—and for so many of us—is boundless.

Charlie Gaddy
WRAL TV Personality
Guilford College Class of 1953

GROWING UP AMONG FRIENDS

"Do you happen to know where Guilford College is?"

Warm afternoon sunlight glinted off the car's windows as the woman who had asked the question perched anxiously at the driver's-side open window. Next to her in the vehicle sat her teenage son. It was a lazy spring afternoon in 1996, and the pair had gotten an early start on visiting a few local colleges and universities in North Carolina prior to the son's senior year of high school. Now, on the fringe of Guilford County, they were lost. "I was hoping to find someone who could tell us," she said with a nervous laugh. The older stranger in the small pick-up truck next to her smiled gently. "*Of all the people she could have asked,*" he chuckled to himself. He then looked her straight in the eye. "I can do better than tell you where it is. I'll show you." With that, the two visitors followed the stranger back to the campus and were treated to a lengthy tour… and a history lesson.

Nearly sixty years before, in September of 1936, Charles Clifford Hendricks and his younger brother Richard set out from their hometown of Archdale, North Carolina and traveled to the campus of Guilford College, located near the city of Greensboro. "Charlie," as he has been known since that time, had graduated from tiny Allen Jay High School the previous spring. Now, as the country regrouped from the Depression and as the world braced for war, Charlie prepared himself for a life of ministry preceded by a brief four-year stop on the grounds of a tiny, quiet school connected with the Society of Friends smack dab in the middle of the Old North State and less than thirty miles from the farm where he had been reared as a child.

Little did he know then that he would never really leave the Guilford campus.

Yet perhaps even that development is of little surprise considering that Charlie grew up in a Quaker family that, as he says, "always believed in education." His own father, Daniel J. Hendricks Sr., attended Guilford for two years after matriculation from his home on old Highway 62 near Archdale. His mother, Sarah Davis, had been a high school graduate in the Center community south of Greensboro. Daniel chaired both the school board and the agricultural committee in Archdale during Charlie's formative years, and at one time Sarah served as president of the local Parent Teachers Association. Amazingly, they remained involved in these community organizations in addition to tending to one hundred twenty-five acres of tobacco as well as eight children—seven of whom attended college at some time or another!

Daniel and Sarah were married in 1914, five years following the death of Daniel's first wife. Eventually, they had six sons and two daughters, with Monroe, being the eldest, having been born in 1902, followed by Aileen (b. 1904), Jay (b. 1907), Bill (b. 1908), Austin (b. 1914), Ruth (b. 1916), Charlie (b. 1918), and Richard (b. 1920). Interestingly enough, five of the children went on to graduate from college between 1922 and 1941, during the largest period of both financial strife and threat of war in American history. (As Lloyd Taylor, Charlie's classmate and friend at Allen Jay notes, "No one gave us a hint that our generation would have the kind of experiences that lay before us in the ten years before and after our graduation"). Charlie himself would later marvel, "during one year there were three of us in college, three of us in high school, and the other two were in grade school." Before Charlie and Richard finished their days at Guilford, Aileen and Ruth both graduated from nearby High Point College, and Monroe completed his studies at UNC-Chapel Hill. Jay also attended High Point for two years, while Bill studied for one semester at

Mars Hill College. As for Austin, though he was the lone sibling not to pursue a level of higher education, he was well known for his mechanical and artistic acumen. When he was eight years old, Austin needed crutches for an injury he had sustained so he fashioned a pair himself out of a nearby Poplar tree.

The Hendricks family lived on a farm in a Quaker community and belonged to nearby Springfield Meeting at which other local Quakers were members. While the cash crop was tobacco, Daniel and Sarah also raised corn and vegetables. All of the boys worked the fields, pulling the tobacco from the long rows, while Aileen and Ruth assisted their mother in the house. The family "was poor but didn't know it," according to Charlie. "In fact, one time I was supposed to bring a dime to school for a weenie roast, but that dime could buy a loaf of bread for the whole family, so I didn't. But we did have three things: clothes, food, and love." Daniel and Sarah owned a six-room house on the land. The house had no electricity, but it did have amenities such as oil lamps and a wood-burning stove. Often the space seemed cramped when all ten members of the family walked about inside. The dinner table in the dining room could only seat eight, so Charlie and Richard often stood during meals. But this closeness also forged a particular bond between Charlie and his brothers. By the time he was born, Daniel was forty-two years old and Sarah was forty, so Charlie found his older brothers were usually the ones who took him to games or played dominoes with him. His younger brother Richard became his best friend, and when Richard skipped the sixth grade, the pair began to walk to school together. Years later, they would spend their first two years at Guilford as roommates.

Of course, existing as the second-youngest child was not always easy either. "Sometimes I got tired of wearing hand-me-downs all the time," confesses Charlie. A story that many of Charlie's friends today still get a chuckle over involves his early clothing. His mother, whom he describes as having creative and unique interests, loved to sew in addition to her summer pastimes of canning beans and picking berries. Often she would make underwear out of flour sacks. Unfortunately, one time she neglected to erase the colored lettering out of a sack. As a result, when young Charlie tried on his pair, the word "plain" was strewn across his backside, while the description "self-rising" adorned his front! Soon though, Charlie started school at Oak Shade Elementary, which was ordinary in its facilities and contained just one outside privy each for boys and girls. In 1928, Oak Shade and Springfield School merged and became Allen Jay High School, which proved to be an early culture shock to the students, as the new school not only provided electric lighting and internal heating, but indoor plumbing as well. Charlie quickly entrenched himself in the life of the high school. "I wasn't the best scholar, but I was a leader." Before his high school years had drawn to a close, Charlie had won a varsity letter in soccer, starred in a play, led student devotions, was elected as a junior marshall, and served as master of ceremonies for the junior-senior banquet. His school spirit and interaction with students and teachers alike at the high school level proved to be a precursor of things to come as a college student—and later, as the 'heart' of the college itself.

Ruth Cross has known Charlie for years. In fact, she met Charlie and Richard, when they all began the seventh grade in 1931 at Allen Jay. "Both were real friendly, and while Charlie was slim, Richard was heavier," confesses Ruth. "Later, I saw that things had changed at our twenty-year class reunion at High Point City Lake—Richard was then slim, and Charlie had gotten heavier." Aside from physical differences, however, it was obvious to Ruth and other classmates that Charlie and Richard were inseparable friends.

"But high school was the time when many things happened in our class," Ruth continues. "We had a Halloween Party in 1935 where we had to meet at the Springfield Church graveyard dressed in white sheets. From there, we were lead to the Jackson home on South Main Street for our party. Just before we graduated we decided to paint the well house with 'Class of '36' in large letters. Charlie held the paint can and I used the brush. Since we were a close-knit class, the rest of the class kept a lookout for teachers. In the years since, Charlie has had many class reunions at his home. He's a wonderful cook and has that smile to give a wonderful welcome. Charlie was my friend in school and will always be a loving friend—so you see why I love Charlie!"

Dave Stanfield, Guilford class of 1944, who later served as pastor of Springfield Friends Meeting in High Point from 1956 through 1961, says of those early years, "I was privileged to know the entire Hendricks family. The family contributed richly to the life and ministries of that Meeting and its community. One of Charlie's special ministries was exercised in the Meeting's kitchen during its annual bazaar. Hundreds of Brunswick stew lunches, dinners, and take-outs bore the distinct flavor of his recipe. (It was a well-guarded secret, so I don't know to this day if it included squirrel, rabbit, possum, or what-all!) Later, Charlie also provided leadership as chairman of the Quaker Lake Board, a summer camp and year-round conference center in Climax, North Carolina that has served thousands of Quaker and other youth in programs and fellowship focusing on a relevant life of Christian faith."

Daniel and Sarah both died two months apart in the fall of 1965, Daniel on September 23rd and Sarah on Thanksgiving night. His mother's death hit Charlie especially hard. Sarah had been active in both the Afternoon Missionary Circle and Women's Missionary Society of Springfield Friends Meeting. She had grown close to Charlie and Richard as they left the safety of the farm and crossed into adulthood. As it was, Charlie got word from Chapel Hill that his mother had finally succumbed to a long illness. Heartbroken in the early morning hours of that November day, he penned his feelings about her, entitled "Thoughts About Mother":

'Ma,' as we so affectionately called her, was a jewel. She was kind, thoughtful, patient, loving, and in all respects Christ-like.

She lived for others and above all for her family. She made a great contribution to the community and the Meeting, for she lived her religion each day.

On this Thanksgiving Day 1965, she has gone to her everlasting home in Heaven. She is now at peace with God as she was with people on earth.

Oh God, I want to thank thee for being her son and pray that I may someday be a small part of what she was and is.

In the last year of her life, Sarah had hosted a Christmas dinner at her house, and twenty-two family members were present. His mother's gathering of family and friends over a holiday meal is just one tradition that Charlie has picked up and continued for decades. These days, Charlie has four nieces—Mary Hendricks Newton, Lydia Hendricks Huoks, Sara Hendricks Clark, and Sue McCulloch—and one nephew—Don Hendricks—who are still living. "But," Charlie points out, "I see Sue, my oldest sister's daughter, often. She lives in Pleasant Garden so we get to eat together occasionally."

Though Charlie has lived by himself since leaving for college, constant reminders of his family and his upbringing are never far, as antiques, family portraits, and old letters decorate his house. "To do what my parents did, putting us all through school during the Depression, well, it was amazing when you think back on it," Charlie says. "They were very special people."

FROM STUDENT TO MISSIONARY...
FOR GUILFORD COLLEGE

As a college student, Charlie took to Guilford like a duck to water almost immediately. Away from home for the first time, his first few days proved to be somewhat overwhelming until he met Seth Macon and Will Edgerton, and the three forged a lifetime friendship. Charlie and his brother Richard had entered the school as recipients of multiple scholarships. Tuition in 1936 totaled less than three hundred dollars, but each Hendricks brother received financial assistance from the college for being in the same family, more for being Quaker students, and a even more for work-study status. In his spare time, Charlie worked in the dining hall, where he washed dishes. "And we had classes for six days a week and had to attend chapel once a day," he recalls. Unlike high school, he didn't have much time for leadership activities. Charlie did audition for the college choir, but "I couldn't carry a tune," he says. When Dr. Wise, the college's music director, heard him sing, the old professor turned and said, "son, sit down." Still, Charlie, Richard, Seth, and Will adapted quickly to Guilford customs, and by the time they watched the football team take on rival Elon College in its annual game at Thanksgiving, they knew that they had fallen in love with their collegiate surroundings. Intent upon becoming a preacher, Charlie began his freshman year as a religion major, but soon he decided to double-major in psychology as well.

After Charlie roomed with Richard, his closest brother and best friend, for his first two years, he lived with a student named James Parker for his third year and then in the home of Dr. Eva Campbell during half of his senior year before he took a semester away from campus. Dr. Campbell was a native of Ohio who had taught at the North Carolina College for Women before coming to Guilford in 1924. A biology professor, she and Charlie grew close even though Charlie never took one of her classes. According to Charlie, "She was a great scholar. To my knowledge, every student she recommended to medical school got admitted. She even took students to our teams' games in her T-model Ford." Charlie became Dr. Campbell's power of attorney in 1947, and the pair remained close until her death in 1982.

As Seth Macon notes, "some of his best stories are about his experiences with women faculty and staff members as he traveled with them and attempted to help them with their personal problems. Anyone can ask him about Dr. Campbell, and then repeat the process by asking about Ms. Milner...Miss Ricks...Maude L. Gainey...Dorothy Gilbert...and others he will name." Charlie admits that he enjoyed "counseling" each of these, but he had two favorite professors in particular during his time on campus. Garness Purdom taught physics and math, while Ernestine Milner, wife of then Guilford president Clyde A. Milner, taught psychology. Charlie found that both were not only gifted teachers but mentors and friends to students as well.

Dr. Purdom was, in Charlie's eyes, "in a class by himself." He garnered respect by the student body and administration alike. "And we, the students, loved him," says Charlie. "Even those he flunked admired him. I flunked his math course, but we remained friends."

Ernestine Milner, meanwhile, helped form perhaps the best tandem in Guilford history. In addition to her teaching duties, Mrs. Milner served as Dean of Women. She even conducted psychology seminars within her home for students once a week. "She helped me understand people better," says Charlie admiringly. "She taught me to value the individual person, a philosophy I later used in my admissions work."

Later, Charlie found two kindred spirits among the faculty in Mildred Marlette and Ed Burrows. Charlie always felt a special affinity for Mildred and Ed because all three had arrived at Guilford as employees at the same time. They all shared observations about the college over the years. As next-door neighbors, Charlie and Ed had things to grumble about occasionally, but basically they cared about each other's well being. In fact, while Charlie has been a life-long supporter of the development of Friends Homes, the three friends agreed that they had mixed feelings about any need to spend the later years as residents in the assisted-living campus. Now Mildred is a resident, and Charlie made sure to escort her tenderly to the memorial service for Ed after he died in December of 1998. The two of them concluded privately during the service that Ed's departure was a pretty dramatic way of avoiding a move to Friends Homes.

Charlie remained in school until 1940, the year he was to graduate. He took time away from school to assist his father as a farmhand. But at the time, World War II raged in Europe, and Charlie was drafted in January of 1941. As a Quaker with Conscientious Objector status, Charlie then left for Civilian Public Service. For six years, he maintained national parks near the Blue Ridge Parkway at Buck Creek Camp, in Marion, North Carolina and in Gatlinburg, Tennessee, as well as at Mount Weather, Virginia. During his service at Mount Weather, he was named assistant director of the camp, a position that called on him to buy and prepare all of the camp's food. "When I was released they gave me a civil service rating, so the government asked me to continue working by maintaining weather maps for the US Weather Bureau," he recalls. He remained there from January through May of 1946. At that point, Charlie was appointed by the American Friends Service Committee to travel to Mexico on a Friends relief project, but once the project expired in September of 1946, he returned to North Carolina. At that point, he served as Executive Secretary of the North Carolina Yearly Meeting Peace Committee, where he remained for one year.

After being hired by President Milner, Charlie registered as a special student for the 1948-49 academic year in order to finish work on his

degree. (Though he was an official member of the class of 1940, he graduated in 1949. Later, as Dr. Milner's nephew Monty Milner would note,
"Charlie would stand not only when his own class was recognized at a
function but for all classes from 1940 through 1949!")

"In 1947, I ran into Dr. Milner in downtown Greensboro," recounts
Charlie. "He touched my arm and asked, 'Charlie my boy, how would you
like to work at Guilford College?' I replied, 'What do you want me to do?'
He let me know that the college was planning to open up a soda shop and
bookstore in an army barrack, and that he wanted me to take charge. I
thought it was a good idea. My starting salary was $2800 per year. When
he told me my salary, he also added, 'Charlie, you do not talk to anybody
about your salary.' Slyly, I responded, 'Don't worry, Dr. Milner. I am as
ashamed of it as much as you are.' While he wasn't as amused about my
comeback as I was, he appointed me as Guilford's first Director of
Admissions five years later."

The soda shop in particular provided students and Charlie alike the
opportunity to get to know one another. Bill Yates, class of 1953, figures
that Charlie was at the center of the campus social structure. "When I
arrived on the Guilford campus in September of 1949, one of the first
people I met was Charlie Hendricks. You knew right away that he was the
manager of the soda shop, which was the social meeting place. Charlie
warmly welcomed new students to campus," Bill says. "Since it was neces-
sary that I worked while in college to help defray expenses, Charlie provided me with a job working in the dining room. I think we were paid
forty cents an hour. Charlie was always willing to help 'his boys.' He would
loan them money, his car (filled with gas), anything. He was the only person on campus that everyone knew would befriend anyone."

Winslow Womack recalls that while Charlie went out of his way to help
students, he also did not let any of them take advantage of his generosity,
either. "One of my first memories of Guilford in any way involves the soda
shop. Just as Charlie completed scooping an ice cream cone for a customer, the student commented that the ice cream cones at Hollowell's
Drug Store at the corner were bigger. Charlie stopped for a moment and

responded, 'If they are so much bigger, why don't you go down there?' Then he asked, 'In fact, why don't you take my car?' With that Charlie reached down into his pocket, pulled out a set of car keys, and placed them on the counter in front of the student. Charlie could give as good as he got, that's for sure."

As he manned the bookstore and soda shop, Charlie found extra time during two summer sessions to head to Europe. He sailed to Holland, to Scotland, and to England during the summer of 1948 to join Friends from across the world at the International Young Friends Conference, which he fondly looks back on "as one of the best experiences of my life." Then, in 1952, he also traveled to the British Isles and Europe with twenty other Quakers to attend the Friends World Conference.

While Charlie had been recruited out high school by, and then worked for, Dr. Milner, he also later worked for his four successors. In fact, Charlie served President Milner for eighteen years, Grimsley Hobbs for fifteen, Bill Rogers for sixteen, Don McNemar for six, and now begins a new tenure for Kent John Chabotar. There may not be any other person in higher education in the nation who can say that they have worked for five of the eight leaders in that school's history. He has performed in a myriad of roles, including running the soda shop and bookstore from 1947 to 1952, serving as Director of Admissions from 1952 to 1967, and then also becoming Alumni Secretary from 1956 to 1958, a position that coincided with a seven-year stint he began in 1956 as Director of Yearly Meeting Relations. In 1963, he was named Head Resident of English Hall, a role that he fulfilled until 1966 ("Mostly," he claims, "I handed out light bulbs and toilet paper"). He served another three-year period as Assistant to the President beginning in 1967, and then worked as Associate Director of Admissions from 1970 until his retirement in 1983.

His retirement, however, was short-lived. At the end of 1983 he returned to the office of admissions as a consultant, until he was named Special Consultant for Institutional Advancement in 1992. He served in that capacity until 1998, when he stepped in as Acting Alumni Director. Since 1999, he has returned to his earlier capacity as Special Consultant for Institutional Advancement.

Charlie credits the Milner presidency with establishing Guilford's reputation as a strong, small, liberal-arts institution. "Clyde Milner served as president from 1934 until 1965 and I have particularly fond memories of him," he stresses. "He and his wife, Ernestine were an outstanding team. They brought in terrific professors, such as Dorothy Gilbert Thorn, Samuel Haworth, Russell Pope, Floyd Moore, Hiram Hilty, Daryl Kent, Curt Victorius, Mildred Marlette, Ezra Weis, and Ed Burrows. He also brought in Herb Appenzeller, who turned Guilford athletics around.

I also served as Dr. Milner's driver when I first came back in 1947. We made many trips together throughout the state. He really had a sense of humor. As we drove home following a speech he had given at a high school commencement, he opened an envelope given to him from the high school. Lying inside was both a five-dollar bill and a ten-dollar bill. He said, 'They probably put the ten dollars in first and after they heard my speech added the extra five.' With a grin, I responded, 'Maybe after they heard your speech, they took out the other five dollars.' We shared a good laugh over that all the way home."

Beverly Rogers, wife of Bill Rogers, recalls that on many occasions "Charlie has described for Bill and me the times during the Milner presidency when Charlie enjoyed acting as a chauffer for the Milners—neither of whom, curiously, could drive. (Actually, it must have been a great time saver to read, write, and talk with each other while Charlie navigated the way.) Not only did Charlie learn all about the inner workings of the college and the important outreach to friends and Friends, but Clyde and Ernestine also must have learned a great deal about the families and alums throughout North Carolina that Charlie knew so well."

Traveling with the Milners provided some levity as well. Once, Charlie and Dr. Milner drove to New York so that Dr. Milner could attend a speaking engagement. In those years the pair shared the same hotel room in order to save the college some money. "Our routine became so that each morning Dr. Milner would rise out of bed first and I would then follow," Charlie remembers. "When it was time for me to dress on this particular occasion, I saw that he was wearing my pants and was ready to head out the door. I bravely pointed this out to Dr. Milner, who laughed and then gave me my pants back."

According to Charlie, Dr. Milner had a sense of humor that could be appreciated by all Guilfordians. Once, in 1959, the Green Bay Packers practiced on campus before an exhibition game in Winston-Salem. Green Bay was one of the best teams in the National Football League in the 1950s and 60's, coached by the famous Vince Lombardi. As the Packers warmed up, Dr. Milner approached Herb Appenzeller, Guilford's coach at the time, and the two watched silently for a few minutes on the sidelines. Finally, Dr. Milner turned and gasped to Coach Appenzeller, "Oh, I believe we are going to have a good ball club this year."

To demonstrate how beloved the Milners were at Guilford, Charlie reflects upon a speech given in 1965 by Tom Taylor as the Milner era came to a close. Tom, the student body president at the time, was and continues to be a close friend of Charlie's. The Milners had a profound effect on Guilford's advancement, and Tom's words that day seemed to Charlie to express perfectly the impact that they made upon each and every student:

"The legacy of stories left by Dr. and Mrs. Milner will, without a doubt, enliven the tradition of this institution for years to come...I have never known a Guilfordian who has not been proud of the dignified personage of Dr. Milner. To us students, you, Dr. Milner, are the epitome of a college president, from your dark blue suit to your silver hair, from your academic bearing to your diplomatic ease and sense of humor in front of an audience...It is even more difficult to explain the students' feelings for you, Mrs. Milner. All of us, who have studied under your guidance and have been counseled by you, realized the sincere interest that you have in your students... ."

Grimsley Hobbs took the reigns after the Milners retired in 1965, and a year later Charlie moved out of English Hall and into the house on Arcadia. At the time, he didn't think he wanted to leave the residence hall, a place where he had mentored many students, but he recognized that it was the best move for him. He became the assistant to Dr. Hobbs, and was quickly put in charge of social events and represented the school at Quaker gatherings, funerals, and inaugurations. To Charlie, Grimsley

Hobbs was not very personable, but he had a solid administration around him and his fifteen-year tenure was highlighted by several key additions to the college, including an expanded library, a thicker curriculum, more faculty members, and the construction of Bryan and Binford residence halls. "While Dr. Hobbs and I did not have the same relationship as Dr. Milner and I had," confesses Charlie "we did find some common interests as time passed. I discovered he also enjoyed antiques, so we spent some days talking about our own collections. I also found that I enjoyed visiting his old mill. Though I felt Dr. Hobbs and I were never on the same wavelength, I did run into him several years ago at a Greensboro carwash, prior to his untimely death. As I prepared to wash my truck, I was stunned and pleased when he thanked me for all I had done for Guilford and for my work in admissions in North Carolina. Suffice to say, those words meant a lot to me."

Of course, in addition to his regular responsibilities during his time on campus in the Milner and Hobbs years, Charlie continued to serve as a valuable advisor to students, many of whom he had admitted to the school personally. He cajoled some, was gentle with others, but mainly, he gave his honest opinion when his guidance was sought. "I recall many pleasant memories involving Guilford College and Charlie Hendricks," says Howard Coble, class of 1958 and now a United States Congressman. One experience I recall vividly involved a final examination for which I was awarded a 'C.' I had prepared well for the exam and had written what I believed was a solid 'B,' and albeit a long shot, an unlikely 'A.' Needless to say, I was crestfallen when I learned of my grade. Later that day I had an occasion to be in Charlie's office. I used Charlie as my personal chaplain and shared with him my disappointment in the grade. Upon completion of my diatribe, Charlie responded in his terse, inimitable manner, 'Coble, let's face it, you *are* a C student.' As I trudged back to my Cox Hall dorm room, I realized that Charlie was probably correct and thereafter warmly embraced the 'C' grades that were not infrequently awarded."

"My favorite Charlie story?" asks Kenny Browning, class of 1968 and now an assistant football coach at the University of North Carolina. "There are too many to decide. Charlie is a great friend with an unbelievable memory. He recruited me out of high school when he was the residence counselor in English dorm. Every day around him was a learning experience."

Kenny's classmate, Henry McKay, agrees. "I have so many fond memories of Charlie and his extended family—the great breakfasts, super desserts, an always-full house—that picking one is difficult," admits Henry. "In the summer of '67, he admitted six student-athletes to the Hendricks' bungalow. Friendships were forged then that still exist over thirty years later. Though we didn't see much of Charlie that summer— he was preparing for the incoming freshman class—he treated us all equally special. He taught us all valuable lessons beyond the classrooms, and the best one that I learned is that 'giving is the gift.'"

"I met Charlie soon after arriving at Guilford in 1975," says Peter Reichard, class of 1980. "I shared a Thanksgiving dinner with him and his neighbor, Ed Burrows, my sophomore year. I nearly always found an excuse to drop by Charlie's house around dinnertime every night. A couple of years later he gave me a T-shirt for Christmas that had the words 'Hey Charlie' on the front and 'What's for dinner?' on the back. Of course, I also recall how he cared for his brothers, Austin and Richard, and sister, Ruth in a very deep way."

Bob Newton, class of 1958, has had a myriad of connections with Charlie. "He gave me an admission tour and then helped me get a journalism scholarship because there was no football money left that year. In the fifties, he lived in the dorm and was a friend to us all. I lived in Thorne House with Charlie and others in the summer of 1957. Then, I was the first occupant of his house in 1960-61. Charlie was an usher in my wedding that same year. Later, he helped me when I was employed at Guilford and then advised me when I was Alumni Association President." Charlie's influence on Bob even stretched far enough that Bob followed in his footsteps by becoming Guilford's Director of Admissions in the 1960s.

Marianna Edgerton, who was a classmate of Charlie's at Guilford, notes "One evening after dinner, probably in our freshman year of 1936-37, I accepted Charlie's invitation to go to Clyde's for a Coca-Cola. Clyde's was just across Friendly Avenue from the college gate and was a favorite hangout for students who could afford soft drinks at a nickel apiece during those Depression years. While we were sipping our Cokes, Charlie confided to me that his goal in life was to be a missionary. I have thought about this many times since and have concluded that Charlie certainly achieved his goal, as a missionary for Guilford College!"

During the 1940s, while Charlie began his career in higher education, more than a few Guilford students got to know him through his work at the Quaker camp at Lake Singletary. Cornelia Coffield Warlick was not only a camper, but she had also known Charlie as a child. "One of my earliest recollections of Charlie was around 1940 when we traveled to eastern North Carolina for church camp. I was a camper and Charlie was a counselor. We have known each other all my life, having lived in the same community, though Charlie attended Springfield Friends and I was at Archdale Friends Meeting. We were at Guilford together (who wasn't?). Charlie hated washing dishes at the soda shop, so I would wash dishes for him and my wages were comprised of a cup of hot chocolate and a doughnut. He was a great friend to me then as he is now. He has come to our house for New Year's Day dinner for nearly forty-five years. The only two years he missed were when we didn't have it once and another time when he needed to take his parents to Florida. Like many others, two of my sons lived at Charlie's house while students at Guilford. He has been more like a brother to me than just a friend—actually, closer than a brother because we never had a disagreement. He has always been at all our important family functions like weddings, fiftieth anniversary celebrations, graduations, and funerals. It has been an honor and a privilege for my family and I to share a close relationship with Charlie."

"The name 'Charlie Hendricks' is synonymous with Guilford College for my generation!" exclaims Jennie Montgomery, class of 1955. Jennie also attended Lake Singletary as a camper. "As a young Quaker from a small North Carolina town," she says, "I became acquainted with Charlie when I was in the eighth grade and he was a counselor there in 1947. I entered Guilford in 1951 but had become more familiar with Charlie at various youth events during those four years before entering college. He was a unique person—pleasant, shy, behind the scenes and helping perform many duties such as cooking, camping, and so forth—who was a guide to all the young Friends.

In 1951 I yearned to be a part of Charlie's 'inner circle'—a real ego booster, for most everyone valued a special word from Charlie. He was never a man of many words but he was always visible and had a tremendous following. To be his trusted friend was like having a status symbol (which was foreign to Quakers). Charlie stood out as a friend of the students. He ran the soda shop where we all gathered after studying in the library each night. He was always on call to chauffer President and Mrs. Milner to their various functions. He was a dominant figure in the cafeteria and in getting special meals and cookouts organized. Later he ran the admissions office and enriched Guilford's student body by traveling the state and eastern seaboard states inviting students to get the Guilford experience and in doing so contribute to it.

(I, as a girl living in Founders Hall, yearned to be one of Charlie's special friends. Being on the 'outside' felt like being unable to get into a special sorority or fraternity. Not being an athlete or a Hobbs girl seemed to be the bar to admittance—or so I thought!) Amazing how powerful his personality affected Guilford students. It took me years, though, to realize that Charlie was actually shy. We all felt Charlie's presence and he had a sixth sense about those who needed his support, both financially and emotionally. He could be called the 'den mother,' the 'banker,' the 'big brother,' or just plain 'Charlie.' His trust and faith in students never seemed to waver. His loyalties to Guilford were genuine and sincere. His dedication remains just as strong today as ever and it is a 'matter of the heart.'

Working with him for many years on the alumni board has afforded me the opportunity to break that seemingly impenetrable wall and get in the inner circle. Charlie rises to every occasion and often the shy side of him may seem brusque and short, but he is never uncaring. He has earned the respect and accolades of many, great and small, and is surely encompassed in the circle of my special friends. He has lived his life in the shadows of those wonderful old trees at Guilford and planted many 'human seedlings' himself. His legacy will live on forever, as long as the word 'Guilford' is uttered."

While he continued to advise students, Charlie's old-fashioned Quaker values and sense of right and wrong began to have a broad impact within the surrounding Guilford County community as well. Once, on one of his many visits to Quaker Lake, he saw a man who was considered to be a 'fundamentalist' who ran a small store. The man sold tobacco in the shop, and one day he asked Charlie, "Do you think it's wrong to use tobacco?" Charlie responded, "Mister Joyce, you're selling it and by doing so you're encouraging people to use it. What do you think?" The fundamentalist sat silently, pondering the question. The next time Charlie visited the store, the tobacco had been removed from the shelves. Later, in the turbulent 1960's, a nearby Greensboro druggist asked Charlie, "Would it jeopardize my business if I let blacks into the store?" Charlie looked right at him. "I'm not worried about you jeopardizing your business, I'm worried about you jeopardizing your place in Heaven." The next day, the druggist opened his doors to blacks and whites alike.

Dave Stanfield recalls many other moments when Charlie's influence extended beyond just the student body. "He is such a dependable F(f)riend!" he exclaims. "While others eloquently describe Charlie's personal interest in them as prospective and active students at Guilford during his fifty-plus years for service there, as a colleague on the College's staff (1974-1992) I can attest to his many valued friendships among the faculty and administration. For many of us he personified those values of integrity, caring, and good humor for which the College is widely known. One other observation worthy of note is Charlie's role as the College's informal 'host' during the North Carolina Yearly Meeting of Friends' annual session on campus each August. For years he represented Guilford at the monthly Ministers' Association meetings, often rising to the challenge of sustaining a relationship of mutual respect and appreciation between the College's liberal arts perception of life and the ministers' often more conservative defense of public and private morals. "

CHECKING IN AT THE HENDRICKS HILTON

Without a wife or children, Charlie soon discovered that he had plenty of extra space in his house. He began hosting boarders, many of whom were Guilford students. ("Some students had been kicked out of the dorms, but others found that they could not afford to pay room and board on campus," he says.) Longtime friend Joyce Clark lived at Charlie's house for eight years with her husband Dee. "I have millions of stories about living in the barn, which Charlie had converted into an apartment," recalls Joyce. "We lived there from 1964 until 1972 during the school year. Charlie always had a waiting list of people who would move in as soon as graduation was over. We just poked our personal belongings in the attic and pulled them out in September when Guilford opened for the fall term.

During the first snowstorm in the barn, we awoke to snow-covered pillows, curtains billowing straight out, and only towels and underwear to stop up the cracks. It was so colorful and all our friends loved the way we decorated. Charlie's car horn also froze and started blowing at three in the morning. When we brought our son home from the hospital in March of 1972, Charlie was standing in the snow taking the most valued of all out pictures—Perry's arrival home in the barn! Charlie was the only person who knew we were going to adopt a baby, as my husband had gone straight to him when we first heard about the possibility. Our love and respect for Charlie's judgment has always paid-off, but never as much as with our son. Living in the barn was the happiest time of our lives. If my husband were alive today, he would say that Charlie was his best friend and that life in the barn was wonderful."

Jim Malone and his wife Shari were two of those folks on Charlie's summer waiting list during the years that Dee and Joyce Clark lived in the barn. Jim and Shari arrived at Guilford in the summer of 1968, newly married and Jim fresh with a masters degree. "The environment at Guilford was reinforcing for us," remembers Jim. "I was still battling my draft board, and had spent the previous seven years at Kent State, which was about to explode. I worked with the American Friends Service Committee in my 'spare' time, and had the opportunity to work with a number of students through this venture. My wife had not completed her degree at Kent State, so she picked up her education at Guilford, graduating in 1970. We lived in Charlie's barn during the summer of '70, before heading off to Virginia Tech to pursue a doctorate. Shari's wonderful experience at Guilford enabled her to get the position as costume designer in the theatre department at Tech. In a trip to the west coast a few years later, we stayed with Charlie so we could fly out of Greensboro. But by then, the barn was gone. We got to know Charlie almost immediately upon arrival at Guilford. His dinners were legendary, and his knowledge of the history of Guilford was wonderful for two Yankees transplanted into such a remarkable community. I don't really have a favorite Charlie story, but will always remember him as a person who exemplified the Quaker spirit (both my wife and I had many Friends in our families). Through Charlie, I met many new people in Greensboro, and had opportunities to meet many others outside the area."

Jeff Kloss, class of 1992, lived with Charlie for three years. "I remember the first time I saw Charlie," Jeff laughs. "I was working the phones of a telethon trying to drum up some interest in the choir tour later that spring. There was Charlie talking up a storm, he just seemed to know everyone. He spoke so loud and everyone he called was his best friend. Then he would begin laughing at some inside joke from forty years ago, I imagine. How odd, this old man sitting in a room of college kids, what a

curiosity, a relic from a bygone era. As I got to know Charlie better and better over the years, I often thought back on that first meeting and had to laugh to myself. Yes, Charlie is a precious antique, but he is never out of place at Guilford. He was right at home there in the telethon, because Charlie has always been active in every aspect of the school.

During the choir trip, Charlie and I got acquainted. For some reason, Charlie took a liking to me and had invited me to a number of his famous breakfasts. It was over one of these meals that I told Charlie I would not be able to return to Guilford because my father had lost his job, and Guilford was too expensive. That was when 'Mr. Guilford College' rolled into action. He asked me a simple question, 'If you could afford Guilford, would you stay?' 'Of course,' I replied. That was all Charlie needed to hear and he set things into action.

Ed Lowe, the music director, told me that I qualified for a Choir Scholarship and would be receiving additional funds the following year. Charlie then asked if I would consider living with him at his house just off of campus. I said I would, but there was a new dean of student life who was strict with the rules. One of the toughest mandates that particular year was that off-campus housing was reserved strictly for upperclassmen and that freshmen and sophomores were not eligible. I put my request in to move off-campus and was denied immediately. I let Charlie know, as he seemed to know a few people in high places. At the time I was rather naive and didn't fully understand Charlie's influence and position as 'Mr. Guilford College.'

Early into the summer I received a telephone call from a very angry administrator. He reluctantly allowed me to move off campus to live with Charlie. He said he didn't know how I did it, but even the President's wife, Beverly Rogers, called to request I be allowed to live with Charlie. He ended the call with, 'I'll allow this one, but I'll be watching you.' I'm not sure where he is today, but I know Charlie is still at Guilford. I'll wager he still gets his way too.

If were not for Charlie, I would not have been able to remain at Guilford."

Others who have who have resided at the famous 'Hendricks Hilton' over the years include:

William Abernethy, Class of 1957; David Addison, Class of 1994; Clay Alexander; Bookie Binkley, Class of 1966; John Brooks, Class of 1968; Ken Browning, Class of 1968; John Newton Cheek; Geoff Clark, Class of 1974; Jock Cofield; Hodgin Cofield; Paul Coscia, Class of 1991; Aaron Denton, Class of 2000; Sayde Dunn; Richard Ewell, Class of 1995; Ed Fellers, Class of 1968; Bill and Pam Fleming, Class of 1976; Donald and Kathryn Ford, Class of 1967; Phil Ford, Class of 1966; Bryan Fulton, Class of 1986; Craig Fulton, Class of 1973; Robert Fulton, Class of 1974; Don Howie, Class of 1984; Craig Jackson; Anthony Locklear; Henry McKay, Class of 1968; Danny McQueen, Class of 1967; Robin McWilliams, Class of 1993; Clyde Milner III; John Morgan, Class of 1969; Bob and Nancy Newton; David Odom, Class of 1964; Jim Pleasants; Bob Rees, Class of 1971; Peter and Linda Reichard, Class of 1979; James Shelton, Class of 1957; Jackson Taylor, Class of 1995; Gary Thompson, Class of 1968; Leon Young, Class of 1968

ANTIQUE BUYING WITH CHARLIE

One day, Charlie took the short walk home from his campus office for lunch and found two women sitting in his living room that he did not recognize. After all three introduced themselves, one of the ladies asked, "What time do you open?" Charlie replied, "Open for what?" Confused, the visitor asked, "Well, isn't this an antique shop?" Charlie smiled, shook his head, and they left.

Those who have lived at Charlie's house at one time or another have acclimated themselves to the vast expanse of antiques either displayed or stored throughout the house—including guest bedrooms, living room, and most notably, the basement. Don Howie claims that as retirement neared for Charlie in the early 1980s that his Arcadia Lane home situated near the Binford Hall entrance to campus grew chock-full of his possessions. Of course, while Charlie is not certain when the passion began, he grew up in a house full of items that the family had collected over the years.

However, his own thirst for collecting didn't develop until he began traveling for Guilford. Free afternoons between college-day programs were spent window-gazing in various antique shops. "There were very few between Asheville and Wilmington that I didn't stop in at least once," Charlie notes. When his parents died, he received some pieces that no one else in the family wanted... until Charlie re-finished them! His great-grandfather, Francis Simpson Davis, had left him a trunk, while Charlie then bought a sideboard that had once belonged to his great-grandmother Hodgin. Soon enough, he picked up a bed that had been his grandparents', along with a corner cupboard that his grandfather Hendricks made. His mother's family provided him with a grandfather clock that they had kept for many generations. A wooden canteen, found with his grandfather's initials on it, is now in Charlie's possession and is valued at eight hundred dollars. In recent years, Charlie has tended to visit many antique malls, although he concedes that, "I haven't purchased many things." Two malls in particular that he enjoys are within easy driving distance in Statesville, North Carolina and Hillsville, Virginia. "Even though I don't need any more items," he admits, "it's hard for me to drive by without stopping."

Even the casual visitor to Charlie's New Garden Road home today cannot help but be amazed at everything that is on display. Shelves of blue glass adorn his windows and walls. Cupboards and chests of all types of wood fill corner spaces. Even a stack of rolling pins rests near the kitchen. "People who come by are usually shocked and say 'I can't believe this,'" laughs Charlie. "And then they spend most of their time here looking around rather than talking to me." Strangers and close friends alike have been known to ask for a tour of the entire house after entering Charlie's driveway entrance and glancing at the assortment of photographs, mantle pieces, and Early American furniture. And the rolling pins? "The reason I started collecting rolling pins was that my mother gave me one that my grandfather had made for my grandmother for a wedding gift in 1876. I now own one hundred and fifty."

The latest appraisal of his broad assortment of antiques falls at a total of thousands of dollars. However, at least some of those pieces came to Charlie, by his own admission, on their way to the junkyard. "Let me give you an example," he explains. "One of the nicest large cabinets I have I first received from Guilford College when they remodeled Duke Hall. It was on the truck to be taken to the dump, so I ran and asked David Parsons, the business manager, if I could take it. I re-finished it and now it sits in my den."

A friend of Charlie's since 1980, Beverly Rogers has gotten to know both him and his most prized hobby perhaps better than anyone else has during that time. As wife of former Guilford President Bill Rogers, Beverly has traveled with Charlie to many functions, such as alumni gatherings and college choir trips. Along the way she has shared his passion for primitive furniture, old buildings, and classic cars. "Charlie's love for the farm he grew up on in Archdale, for old farm buildings and machinery, as well as antique furniture and 'stuff,' has never diminished," she says. "Neither has his sense that a community should know one another and all pull together, just as it had done in the rural setting of his childhood. During trips through Randolph, Guilford, and Alamance counties, Charlie would point out where the old barns and fields had been, where the mills were, where the old general stores had been—he loved the rural landscape, its people, and its history. He and his brother also bought a piece of land up in the mountains with an old house on it. It served as an enjoyable retreat, particularly in the hotter periods of the summer. But eventually it began to feel more like work going up there, and Charlie seemed to relish his invitations to go to someone else's beach or mountain home even more. In recent years he ventured to Maine, Maryland, and western North Carolina, so there was not much call to his old mountain home. It was sold.

Then of course, there was Charlie's small bungalow, garden, and outbuildings on Arcadia Drive. He filled every inch of the walls, closets, attic, and garage with antique dishes, glassware, copper and brass, and memorabilia of all sorts, such as his Aunt Ann's old hearing trumpet. The house got so full that it almost burst. When the opportunity came to purchase the big two-story house on the corner of New Garden Road directly across from the college entrance, Charlie snapped it up. Friends like Clarajo Pleasants helped him get re-settled and decorated, which was no small task!"

Charlie's current house also boasts old quilts and several antiques from Dr. Campbell, the biology professor from Ohio. Yet his most prized possession is a family hand-me-down luster pitcher. One day he took his mother to see Aunt Ann, who lived in a log-house in Guilford County. Ann announced, "Sarah, I want you to have this pitcher, and when you are through with it I want Charlie to have it." The pitcher, originally from Wales, is now over three hundred years old.

Two vintage automobiles have also graced the Hendricks driveway over the years, a 1934 Chevrolet and a 1927 T-model Ford. As Beverly Rogers notes, "Charlie has always had a keen eye for automobiles." In fact, Charlie has often lent his classics out for wedded couples to be whisked away to the marital receptions.

"He has been about as loyal to certain cars as he has been to Guilford College," admires Beverly. "Not only did he love driving the Chevy himself, but he also surprised a number of students like Curt Hege by loaning it out for dates and other journeys. When the car turned fifty, he took the classic in for new paint, and then decided to do a full restoration. A year or two later, he got his Chevy back. For a price, not only had it been restored, but modified! In fact, some observers thought the staid, conservative car now looked like hot-rod. But Charlie knew what he was doing. Now he had a sharp buggy that would really turn heads—painted in Guilford colors no less, maroon and gray. It now has a modern roadworthy frame, hydraulic brakes, a big 356 V8 engine with special carburetor, a custom dash, carpeting, low profile chrome spoke wheels, and a smooth-sounding muffler. In the early 1990's, Charlie and Bill drove over together to Wilkesboro to an auction that was disposing of some sixty cars from an antique auto museum. It was all they could do to leave without Charlie bidding up too high on two snazzy '65 Ford Thunderbird convertibles, one apple red and one blue."

CUTTING DOWN THE NETS

Though Charlie did not continue his soccer career beyond his playing days at Allen Jay High School, he has remained a big sports fan. He still drives to Chapel Hill every fall to watch a season's worth of football games at the University of North Carolina, and he followed Wake Forest's basketball program with enthusiasm and pride when his good friend Dave Odom coached there. However, as one might guess, he bleeds deepest for his alma mater. By his own rough estimate he has now attended over six hundred Guilford basketball games and over three hundred in football. In 1964 he traveled to Cullowhee to cheer the Quakers as they ended Western Carolina's home winning streak in football. He can still recite the starting five on the 1973 N.A.I.A. basketball championship squad: seniors M.L. Carr and Teddy East, junior Greg Jackson, sophomore Ray Massengill, and freshman Lloyd "World" Free. Amazingly, three of those players, Carr, Jackson, and Free, went on to play in the N.B.A.

While the '73 team was talented, Charlie revels in the fact that Guilford was not a seeded team entering the tournament yet still won it all. Though he never played the game himself, Charlie may have had a hand in the Quakers' tournament run psychologically. "I, as well as others, followed the 1972-73 championship team throughout the year and through the tournament run in Kansas City," he recalls. "While we were in Kansas City, I was walking with M.L. Carr and told him that if we won the national championship, I would buy him a new pair of shoes that he had been eye-ing. Well, on the Saturday before the final M.L. said, 'Charlie, let's go ahead and buy those shoes because we are going to win tonight.' We went ahead and got them and later that night we won. I guess you could say that I made a contribution to the championship," he says with a chuckle. Dennis Haglan, another prominent Guilford coach at the time, does not recall Charlie being as confident of victory, however. "Of course, several things stand out about this trip," notes Dennis. "Four of us, including Charlie, were usually packed into a hotel room so that we could save money. It was like being a kid again. At Municipal Auditorium, Charlie always walked the concourse every time a game would get close. Each of us would sit in separate seats since there were spare rows for most games, excluding the championship. Charlie would sit behind me and near the top row. I would turn to speak with him about the game, and he'd be gone. Once we re-took the lead, there he was again, back in his seat. This went on for the entire week. He was always disappearing during the close moments, as if he became 'Casper the Ghost.'"

Primarily, Charlie credits three men for Guilford's rise to athletic prominence during the Milner and Hobbs presidential era: basketball coaches Jerry Steele and Jack Jensen, and the longtime athletic director, Herb Appenzeller. Steele, who later coached the A.B.A. Carolina Cougars and at High Point University, began to build the Quakers into a power dur-ing the 1960's. Jensen, who directed the '73 title, also guided the Quakers to two national championships in golf. Appenzeller served as athletic direc-tor for thirty-one years in addition to his tenure as football coach.

Jerry Steele and Charlie often traveled together in Charlie's car to visit prospective recruits. In 1964, the pair drove to the town of Enka outside of Asheville to see an outstanding prospect named Leon Young. While they spoke with the high school senior about coming to Guilford, Leon's younger brother got thrown from a pony into a manure pile. "Jerry picked the injured boy up and we took him on to the hospital," remembers Charlie. "After it turned out he hadn't been hurt too badly, I advised Jerry

to send a box of candy to the Young family once we returned home." Four
years later, Young graduated from Guilford.

By the dawn of the 1970's, Charlie had grown close to other Guilford
staff members, especially the coaching staffs and their spouses. Dennis
Haglan recalls how Charlie not only hosted their respective teams for special dinners but also invited coaches' families for specific outings. Dennis
particularly savors the coaches-only meals Charlie served. "During my
first tenure at Guilford," he recalls, "Charlie would have the coaches over
for lunch or dinner on numerous occasions; he always had fresh vegetables. He *always* had the best corn on the cob, peach cobbler, applesauce,
etc. For a long while he owned a home in the mountains of Virginia. It did
not have heat or running water, but what it did have was character and a
lovely mountain setting. One year he invited the coaches and some other
friends to join him for Thanksgiving there. That was one of the most special Thanksgivings my wife Patti and I ever had!" Sheila Kendall Dunning,
class of 1971, laughs at the memory of another Thanksgiving when
Charlie hosted coaches from several teams to his sometimes-vacant
mountain home. "We were all there in the Virginia hills," she says. "All the
coaching staff and families had been invited up for lunch. Charlie's directions were simple—'Go till you think you've gone too far, and then keep
going!' When we arrived we discovered that the house had been closed up
for some time and we found that many dead flies lay in the windowsills.
'Don't worry about those now,' Charlie advised. 'Let's get the groceries
unloaded, the fire going, and the wood-stove fired up first.' We conceded
and began taking care of the chores. All of a sudden we realized that all
those dead flies weren't dead after all. The heat from the fireplace had
brought them back to life and they swarmed the single light bulb hanging
in the main room. We started to swat at them, but Charlie said, 'Don't do
that...I've got some bug spray that will kill 'em.' He rushed to the cabinet,
pulled out a can, and promptly sprayed the light bulb with oven cleaner!
The spray foamed and hissed, but it did the job just the same. We all had
a good laugh over his ingenuity."

Even today, Charlie serves breakfasts to a variety of Quaker teams. Barb Bausch, the Quakers' highly successful women's basketball coach, emphasizes, "Charlie has been a big supporter of athletics at Guilford College for probably as long as he's been here." Though he preferred to follow the men's teams over the years, particularly in light of the '73 basketball team, Charlie gained a new interest in the women's basketball team when Chris Kosiba, class of '97 and a former player on the men's team, began to work with him on admission tours in 1999. "Chris was an assistant coach to me at that time," says Barb. "So, while Charlie groomed Chris in the fine art of recruiting, Chris urged Charlie to come see the women's team play. He did, and ever since he has been a big fan and friend of the team. The girls have been blessed with meals and good fellowship at his house to prepare for games, to kick off new seasons, and to celebrate championships and graduations. He has taken a keen interest in the student-athletes as people. It has meant a great deal to me to know a man of such loyalty and enthusiasm for an institution and its people. He has renewed my spirit on several occasions, and he always brings a smile to my face when I receive a call, see him in the stands, receive a card, or cross paths on campus. I hope we have provided him with the same spirit, enthusiasm, and encouragement. Thanks Charlie!"

Jack Jensen knows that Charlie's enthusiasm is nothing new to Quaker sports. "Charlie would serve meals to our basketball team, particularly fantastic breakfasts before our team left for the airport to play in the NAIA Tournament in 1966, 1967, 1968, 1970, 1973, and 1976. And of course, my other memory of him was captured on film forever. On St. Patrick's Day, March 17th, 1973, Guilford won the NAIA basketball championship in Municipal Auditorium in Kansas City. As strands of the net were being cut down, 'Mr. Guilford College' was hoisted on the shoulders of players to cut down his piece. It was a truly great moment... a great person sharing a slice of Guilford College history."

FRATERNITY OF PROFESSIONALS

It was the early 1990's, and Bob McLendon, the Director of Admissions at Brevard College, was exhausted. He needed a break. He needed a vacation from admissions, from the 'life on the road' recruiting high school students, from the organization known as CACRAO, and from everything else related to his profession. So he and his wife took a three-week trip out to quiet countryside in Washington state for some rest and relaxation and the opportunity to detach from everything back in North Carolina for a little while.

One morning while the McLendons were there, Bob ventured down to a nearby lake. A born fisherman, he relished the chance to get a few casts in during his respite. As he approached the water's edge, there was not a soul within shouting distance except for a man with a small rowboat. The man noticed the rod in Bob's hand and asked if he wanted to join him, as he too had planned a day of fishing in the middle of the lake. Bob agreed, and they silently rowed their way out onto the water.

After some time of waiting for a fish to bite, the stranger asked Bob where his home was. After Bob answered, the man looked at him for a moment and said, "North Carolina, huh? Never been there myself. Only person I know there is Charlie Hendricks."

Slack-jawed in disbelief, Bob McLendon dropped his head, let out a chuckle, and reeled in his line.

Since 1952, it has been through his valuable and dedicated work in college admissions that folks outside of the immediate Guilford connection (and even across the country) have been able to introduce themselves to Charlie. Such is the case with Esther Cummings. While Esther and her husband Ralph have now known him for several decades, she confesses, "My first impression of Charlie was not a good one. I was secretary to the Dean of Men at Guilford in the early in the 1960s. One day the old wooden floor outside the door of my office in Old Memorial Hall began to squeak from heavy footsteps. The door flew open and someone from the nearby registrar's office began to say, 'Here he comes, here comes Charlie.' The next thing I heard was a firm voice saying, 'Mrs. Thompson, you take care of the registrar's office and I'll take care of admissions.' He turned and left, slamming the old half-glass door that barely withstood the pressure. There was no doubt in anyone's mind that Charlie had made his point. As I became better acquainted with Charlie, I realized I had never met anyone like him. The entire admissions staff consisted of one secretary and him. He lived and breathed Guilford College. He was extremely interested in others. He worked so hard, yet I never once heard him complain."

Charlie has been to every high school in North Carolina at some time or another, and over the years he's grown close to many high school counselors, including Evelyn Harris. Evelyn, who counseled students at High Point Central High School for twenty-eight years, emphasizes the impact he made on nervous students who were unsure of their college potential. "One statement stands out describing Charles Hendricks," she notes. "He has been a friend to his professional associates, but also to students. I met Charlie at a College Day Program in 1962 at a time when College Day was an unpleasant experience for high school counselors because college admissions was so competitive and the admissions people did not hesitate in telling students that admission to a particular school was not likely. Charlie never approached students with a negative attitude, but rather one of being helpful. He sent students to other admissions counselors if Guilford was not a possibility. That day in 1962, I realized that this was a special person who believed that every person had special worth.

Our friendship was further nurtured by Charlie's action of inviting me to go in the van to conferences and to professional meetings. I found out that he was a collector of friends and have never ceased to be amazed that no matter where I was when I was that someone would know him. Charlie was a stabilizing force in my career, and he helped me learn and understand the admissions process. My friendship with Charlie did not end with my retirement but has continued into its fourth decade. I look forward to breakfast at Charlie's twice a year. When I think of all the young people he has helped professionally, of the time he has spent cultivating friendships, of the impact he has had on Guilford College, I feel privileged that our paths crossed because he has certainly had a positive impact on me."

In those years, college reps often stayed the entire day at the particular high school they were visiting. As a result, lunch was always served, and the reps eventually got to know one another fairly well. While the bonding among counselors was easy, actually luring students to attend Guilford in those days proved to be simple in some locations but difficult in others. Students across southeastern states tended to show serious interest in the school, while recruiting in northern states was restricted mostly to Quaker prep schools. "Our biggest competitors back then were UNC-Chapel Hill, East Carolina, and Elon," Charlie recalls. Locally, school systems in Salisbury, Winston-Salem, Raleigh, and Durham arranged to have college counselors visit every year. "However," Charlie notes, "there were not many high school guidance counselors back then. English teachers often performed some of the guidance duties. As a result, sometimes I spoke in English class…and even chapel."

Life on the admissions circuit, which became known as being 'on the road,' proved to have its adventures. "One time I asked Ed Burrows to go to a college day program in my place down east," laughs Charlie. "When he returned, he walked up to me and said, 'Charlie, you keep your job and I'll keep mine.' I guess I didn't realize how tough it was. A counselor said to me once that she didn't know if she had anyone that was 'good enough' to come to Guilford. I told her, 'have 'em apply and let me make that decision.' And I ended up looking at each student's application with a careful eye."

At least a handful of students that Charlie talked to developed into interesting cases along the way. Once, he decided to turn down a student from Morehead City named Danny McQueen. "But then he came back and gave me a sob story. I could see his potential so I re-evaluated my previous decision," he admits. "Now, Danny runs one of the largest furniture stores in the southeast." After Charlie recruited Charlie Gaddy to campus, he realized the freshman needed a job, so he set him up in the dining hall. "But I had to keep on him because he talked to all the girls." Another year, a student arrived at Guilford from Goldsboro and played in a football game for the Quakers without even registering. When Charlie approached him, the student responded that the coaches had told him to 'come on up.' Dryly, Charlie answered him. "Well, you better apply first."

Dave Odom, who has coached basketball at both Wake Forest and the University of South Carolina, recalls his first contact with Charlie, one that provided Dave with quite a shock. "First impressions usually are lasting impressions and true. Such was the case when I was a senior at Goldsboro High School," remembers Dave. "My mother, who was a nurse doing private duty at the time, decided I would go to Guilford College upon graduation in the spring of 1960. Accordingly, I applied to the Director of Admissions, who was Mr. Charles Hendricks. He was a committee of one, the sole voice on such matters. After a couple of weeks, the long awaited reply and answer to my application arrived. The letter was signed by Charles Hendricks and was polite, short, and to the point—my request for admission had been denied.

My mother was angry yet determined. I was hurt and unsure. Mother's patient at the time was Elton Warrick, a Board of Trustees member, a Quaker, and known to be 'Mr. Guilford College' by all accounts at the time. He read Mr. Hendricks' letter to me, instructed my mother not to worry and two days later a note from Mr. Hendricks came to me explaining that my application had been reconsidered and that he was pleased to offer me admission to Guilford College. It was signed 'Charlie'... I learned that was how he was known to both friends and those connected to Guilford.

Charlie was and still is my friend. He was a mentor to many and a special friend to the lucky few who lived in his midst in English Hall. He gave me an opportunity, a chance to prove myself when conventional wisdom said otherwise. Charlie, I hope you feel you made the right decision... on second thought!"

Like Dave Odom, Bill Wearmouth didn't know what to think when he first met Charlie in 1957. "A Guilford alum, whose name I cannot remember," says Bill, "had told my family of this Quaker school near Greensboro. Not only was it an excellent liberal arts college, but tuition and fees totaled $800 per year and that made it doubly attractive. So on the day after Christmas, not thinking that it could be anyone's vacation time, the alumnus and I drove from South Carolina and, ultimately, down this beautiful avenue of cedar trees lining the road from Jamestown to Guilford. We were met by a Mr. Charles Hendricks, who, allegedly, was in charge of the school's admissions. I never saw an office, a business card, or any credentials confirming his claim. He looked more like an astronomer or a history professor. There were no forms to be completed or any questions asked of me. In fact, the 'interview' consisted of a stroll around the campus with Charlie and the alum deep in conversation, while I kept a dutiful and silent five paces to the rear. Seldom in my life have I been so ignored. Later I learned that Charlie—not Chuck and never Chaz—had built his technique based on his experience and education. More likely, he had been mad about having to give up a day of vacation. By the end of the day, I had been accepted to Guilford as a transfer for the following month. It is a mystery he may someday clear up for me.

During the next year and a half, I found that Charlie had a rare personality trait. In my lifetime I have met a handful of people who, for some reason, have the ability to make people think that they are that person's best friend. I know better now, but back then even though I knew he had plenty of friends, he made me feel special. As testimony of how loyal he is to his friends, Charlie has tracked me down by phone on December 26th—the day of our first meeting—for forty-five consecutive years. It underlies what a true friend (and Friend) he has always been."

Mary Bland Josey, a colleague of Charlie's who worked in admissions at Meredith College in Raleigh, recalls the formation of what eventually became the North Carolina Post-Secondary Committee of CACARO (Carolinas Association of Collegiate Registrars and Admissions Officers). "In the spring of '52 or '53, some schools in western North Carolina invited colleges to send representatives to talk with interested college-bound high school seniors," Mary says. "Then, one or two days later, a similar program was held way "down east." This created a traveling nightmare for that period of time. So four college reps—Charlie, Bill Brinkley of Duke, Edith Kirkland of Salem, and Charles Phillips of what is now known as UNCG—eventually met together in the lobby of the Virginia Dare Hotel in Elizabeth City. Together they realized that some coordination was needed and all agreed to Bill's suggestion that he approach the North Carolina Colleges Conference about the need for a state committee of college personnel to coordinate the annual schedule for these events in the high schools. The NCCC agreed and Bill Brinkley became chairman of this new committee, serving for ten years."

As a result, Charlie was elected as CACRAO's very first president, a position he filled for the 1971-72 term. Since that year, he has been an honorary member of the organization, which has bestowed upon him several awards, including the creation in 1995 of the Charles C. Hendricks Award, given at the annual conference to the CACRAO member who does the most behind-the-scenes work without being an elected official. On December 5th, 2001, CACRAO held Charlie Hendricks Day at its 30th annual conference in Charlotte. Additionally, Charlie garnered recognition in 1976, when school counselors in North Carolina voted him as the top admissions official in the state, and in 1982, when he received the Distinguished Service Award from the Southern Association of College Admissions Counselors.

While Charlie remains proud of these accomplishments, he is quick to point out that the friendships formed with counselors from all backgrounds have meant much more to him. Rosalie Adams is one such friend. Rosalie, a longtime guidance counselor at West Forsyth High School, has this to say. "There are so many things to say about this dear man. Those of us who have known him all these many years could each probably fill volumes of stories about him," she claims. "Two of my favorite stories concern food. At a time when Charlie was not exactly hitting it off with Grimsley Hobbs, the higher administration at Guilford held a meeting of high school counselors on the campus. At the break, I met Charlie outside of the building in which we were meeting. After a few pleasantries, he asked where the group was having lunch, and when. Well, when I told him we knew of no plans for lunch he turned pale and left! At the end of the meeting that followed, as we were being wished a safe trip home, Charlie appeared and asked permission to make an announcement. The announcement was that we were all being served lunch at his home in fifteen minutes. From the time he had seen me during the break until the time of his announcement, he had decided on a menu, bought the food, rounded up some friends to help get things prepared, and was ready to be a gracious host to fifty or so hungry counselors. In the same way, Charlie has met the needs of counselors and the needs of Guilford College time after time after time. He's always known that counselors were his pipeline to the students, and he always treated us with kindness. It never seemed like a business to him!

My second food story has to do with my own office. The counselors in my office just did not seem to be jelling together and working for the same goals. When I talked to Charlie about my concern, he wanted to know what I was going to do about it. I did not know! Finally, I got the idea that we should socialize in some way and that I might take all of them out to dinner. As I discussed this with Charlie, he offered to prepare the meal and serve it in his home. Great idea! We chose the date and I invited everyone in my department as well as their spouses. None of them knew Charlie very well and none of them had been in his home, so I tried to prepare them ahead of time about what they might expect. And you do you do that? Well, the night arrived and everyone showed up. What a feast. Of course, we sat boy-girl at his big dining room table with his elegant cloth and napkins, antique china, glassware, and silver. Charlie himself brought each dish to the table, every time announcing 'those potatoes slept in the ground last night' or 'the apples in that deep dish pie slept on the tree last night.' Such a fresh and refreshing meal! What a way to offer a means for everyone at that table to see things through the same eyes. Afterwards, we all sat around and chatted. We admired Charlie's taste in furnishings and talked about what types of antiques our own grandparents had. As we rubbed our stuffed bellies, we started to realize that we did in fact like each other and were working for the same cause. That night, Charlie had served a secret ingredient—the glue needed to turn my staff into a closer and more effective guidance department."

Dick Baddour, now the Athletic Director at the University of North Carolina, says that "Charlie Hendricks represented who we were, what we were about. He was a professional and a gentleman. We went to those high school programs to provide a service to the young men and women of North Carolina and Charlie knew and taught us that they deserved the best we had...every day. He also taught us how to do these jobs without a competitive spirit and with a strong sense of caring for each other. While Charlie had 'his way of doing things,' his sense of humor carried the day. He always had a story and always told it with a spirit and style—Charlie's style.

One time we were at a restaurant having dinner—maybe ten or twelve people. At the end of the meal when the waitress brought us our check, she said kindly, 'Have a nice day.' When she left Charlie said, 'I may or may not have a nice day. I may not want to have a nice day. It is my business whether or not I have a nice day.' The purpose of the story is only to say that his fundamental belief is that all of us have to determine our own destiny and we responsible for our own 'day.' He is one of the very special people who has made a difference."

George Dixon, longtime Director of Admissions at North Carolina State University, underscores that "Charlie Hendricks is solely responsible for my making the commitment to the admissions professions some thirty years ago...and I have never regretted my decision one time. In the summer of 1974, as a fresh-faced fairly recent college graduate, I had the great fortune of being hired as an Assistant Director of Admissions at NC State University, my alma-mater. Back then, being an assistant director was a glorified way of saying admissions road-runner/recruiter. Part of my training in the profession was to attend the CACRAO Summer Workshop with all of the other new road-runners from colleges across the state. One of the very first people all of the newcomers met was Charlie Hendricks, then the Director of Admissions at Guilford College, CACRAO's first President, and already a legend in the profession. I became known to Charlie first as 'Ken's boy' in recognition of Ken Raab, Charlie's long time friend and the soon to retire Director of Admissions at State, and then I was known as 'Anna's boy,' because Ken's replacement was Anna Keller, the long time NCSU Assistant Director and then new Director of Admissions at State and also a long time friend of Charlie's. I loved being Ken and Anna's boy.

My introduction to Charlie was eye opening...he looked just like the Quaker on the Quaker Oatmeal Box then and now...he was gruff and direct but always with a twinkle in his eye. We quickly learned that Charlie loved Guilford College (his one and only college and employer ever), he loved and valued the important work of an admissions officer, he loved the travel part of our work and learned that being late for anything was tantamount to a cardinal sin....Charlieism's were created: 'being on time always means at least fifteen minutes early'; " you always ride home with the one that 'brung you' (meaning that if you rode anywhere with Charlie, as many of us did, you had better not ride back with anybody else); 'high school counselors are the most important people in the school...always make a point of meeting them and introducing yourself'; 'treat the last student you may see on Friday afternoon just like the first one you may have seen on Monday morning'; 'make friends everywhere you go and you'll never have to eat alone'; 'there must be more Guilford College alums than any other college in the world and Charlie must have admitted them all because no matter where you go someone always calls out 'Charlie...how the heck are you and tell me what's going on at Guilford.'

Charlie taught his many protégée's the true value of friendship, the importance of putting others first, the joy that comes from doing something nice for someone, especially someone less fortunate. Just look at Charlie's life and the many, many friends he has and has had over the years in Friends Home Retirement Center where he visits, grocery shops for, or just takes folks for an outing to break up an otherwise rather drab existence. He is known and remembered by many for many things...opening his home to countless numbers of needy Guilford students...home-roasted peanuts at Christmas, Christmas morning breakfasts for friends and neighbors...how to make sweet tea and apple cobbler...antiques and more antiques...his birthday parties (which you had better not miss because he *never* forgets and will *never* let you live it down)…public speaking filled with more wit and humor than anyone I know…and a constant presence for any number of friends be it at a wedding, first child's christening or birthday, or funeral.

I love Charlie Hendricks and I am a better professional, friend and person because of the life lessons I learned from spending the last thirty years with him. I am proud to count him among my closest friends. My memories of less hectic times going about admissions work with Charlie with names surfacing like 'Teddy Bear' and 'Jarrett House' or 'World of Clothes' and the 'Silver Gull' always bringing a smile…I have been blessed in many ways in my life with Charlie's friendship being one of the very best blessings."

Randy Doss, class of 1982 and the current Director of Admissions at Guilford, says, "When I think of Charlie I think of all the students, school counselors, college admission representatives, and others he has influenced. He certainly can name-drop with anyone. When I see Charlie at CACRAO events, he is never alone! His catch phrases like 'Admissions and farming are just alike, you never catch up,' come out of my own mouth when speaking to others about admissions.

Before I even came to work at Guilford, Charlie had made an impact upon me. While at Greensboro College, I had the opportunity to stand beside him many times at college-day fairs and he always made points to me about admissions, such as when he believed the profession was not held in the highest respect. So many times he impressed upon me that college reps should not sit behind, or leave, their tables at fairs. These comments really demonstrated to me how much the field of higher education meant to him. Through word or by action, I continue to be amazed by how many people have been molded by Charlie."

One of Charlie's closest friends, Jerry Harrelson, class of 1972 and now the Director of Alumni Relations at the College, is the rare Guilfordian who did not happen to cross paths as a student with Charlie. "In my case," Jerry confesses, "I can honestly say I never heard the name Charlie Hendricks during my tenure at Guilford College from 1967-1972. I was busy being a college student in Yankee Stadium/Cox Hall and ultimately marrying Melissa Thompson in 1970 and moving from Bryan Hall to number twenty-eight Frazier Apartments. After graduation, and a brief active duty assignment with the Army Reserve and graduate school, I joined UNCG and spent the first 30 years of my career in undergraduate admissions. That is where I first met Charlie. Our first encounter was to share a room at the Williams Motel in Whiteville, NC while covering an eastern week of high school college days. Per diem rates for both the public and private schools were always sparse and we would always prefer splitting the costs given the modest salaries that were common. This is probably where I first hear the phrase that has stuck in my mind ever since and sometimes plagued me too… "fifteen minutes early is on time". This continues to be Charlie's mantra too.

Fast forward thirty years and I find my energies working for Guilford College as its alumni director. I concluded my tenure with the UNC system in February of 2002 and returned to my alma mater that March. It has been a great experience to now work where I spent the best years of my life. The clothing styles may have changed and there are more parts of bodies pierced than in the Seventies, but the character of what makes Guilford College a special place in higher education still remains. The added benefit has been to be able to once again travel the roads with Charlie and pick his single memory of the thousands of graduates he knows. As Charlie approaches his 85th birthday, he continues to be active and comes to his office most days and when all else fails with respect to an alumni question, a historical issue, who married whom, when did this happen…the memory bank of that fellow next to Charlie Patterson's office always kicks into gear. In all of higher education in the United States, I can say with certainty, Charlie Hendricks is "Mr. Guilford College" and will never be replicated. His long tenure at the college and his work with Clyde Milner, Grimsley Hobbs, Bill Rogers, Don McNemar and now Kent John Chabotar… Charlie occupies a singular position in the state and the nation. Guilford College and the thousands of alumni will forever be grateful for the contributions he has made to the academy and to their lives.

When I think about him during countless occasions when we have shared a meal, walked on the beach, sat through a college day in a hot gymnasium, gone to a Carolina football game, helped move furniture, participated in Homecoming or Alumni Weekends at Guilford, built a lake in Rockingham County, stopped at that flea market or antique shop, picked strawberries, made a road trip to Nashville to surprise Charlie Gaddy, had a coffee at McDonald's, gone to see the Panthers lose another game, spent the weekend at Buffalo mountain, or a myriad of other memorable events that would only go for many more pages, one and only one thing comes to mind.... *Charlie Hendricks is our friend.* Charlie has been our amigo, our confidant, our associate, our ally, and our colleague."

I've been a friend of Charlie's since 1973," concurs Charlie McCurry, "when I was on the admissions staff at UNCG. Charlie was known as the 'Daddy Dean of the Roadrunners' when I started. After every College Day program in North Carolina, we'd all line up behind Charlie in our cars like baby roadrunners to follow him to our next location . . . as he'd been out on the road for so long in North Carolina that he knew the location of every school and antique shop in the state! He was also the unofficial keeper of the 'Code of Ethics' for all college reps.

Charlie was the speaker at the CACRAO Conference in Myrtle Beach in either 1976 or 1977 and during his speech he talked about how he grew up in a poor Quaker family. He told the underwear-flour sack story. He had such a gift of making a crowd, whether it was made up of students or adults, feel comfortable and entertained while he spoke to them. Charlie ate, slept, and breathed Guilford College. He even dressed in the school colors before it was cool to do so. He was always recruiting, even talking to small children about the school! When he'd meet a new youngster that he had heard was smart, he'd always say "we'll have to get you into Guilford." Charlie always stayed at his table during College Day programs, even when he didn't have any students around. He thought it was the professional thing to do, and he would give new reps a hard time if they left their own stations. Admissions rookies and veterans alike had a tremendous amount of respect for Charlie. You wanted to stay on his good side!

My own sense is that Charlie went through some tough professional times at Guilford, particularly when he was no longer director of Admissions. Even during those times, however, he would do anything for the school. He used to talk and laugh about Dr. Hobbs giving a speech once and saying "I stand in reflected pride," in reference to Charlie and his accomplishments.

In 1976, I was looking for a place to live and Charlie helped me find a room in the back of a house in Greensboro with an elderly woman he knew. He helped me move my furniture and clothes and when we were almost through, the woman approached me and exclaimed 'You have too many things!' With that, I knew the living arrangement wasn't going to work so I told her to give me a few minutes and I'd find another place. Immediately, Charlie offered his own house and a room. He told me 'you can stay for a month or so until you find another place.' I ended up living in Charlie's house for the next five years! Needless to say, Charlie was a generous, loving man who was at once friend, father, brother, and jokester. I found in time that he was that way not only with me but with a litany of others as well. Even in his bad moments, Charlie is a friendly dragon... there is fire coming out of his mouth, but if you look around the fire, his tail is always wagging. Come to think of it though, you won't notice the tail because usually his tongue never stops wagging. He could flat talk the bark off of a tree!"

Brad McIlwaine agrees with Charlie McCurry's assessment, noting that he found "the man who really is Mr. Guilford College" to be quite a character when the two first met. "I got to know Charlie after graduation in 1979 when I got a job in the admissions office. He was my boss, supervisor, Quaker mentor," Brad admits. "Now, I look around my house in Winston-Salem and there's not a single piece of furniture that isn't from Charlie, either purchased or given. He not only took me under his wing in admissions, but he introduced me to the world of antiques. He really brought the concept of Quakerism and the spirit of Guilford College home to me after I graduated and was able to become good friends with him. I will forever be one of Charlie's greatest admirers and would do whatever I could if he were to call and ask for any kind of help."

The late Bill Starling, longtime Director of Admissions at Wake Forest, summed his feelings about Charlie by concluding that, quite simply "Charlie is one of the great characters of the world. When I began at Wake

Forest in 1958, he, along with Stan Broadway at High Point College, took me under their wing. He is a walking encyclopedia about so many things. I grew up in eastern North Carolina, and during the confusing period of the 1960's, I struggled with the idea of 'doing what is right.' I really was helped by the Quaker philosophy that was manifested through Charlie.

He is irreplaceable."

Charlie notes that "Two of the most respected and well liked directors of admission are no longer with us — Bill Starling and Jean Rayburn. Everyone admired and loved them, and their deaths were a great loss to our profession. Bill Starling started working at Wake Forest University two or three years following his graduation as an admissions counselor. He worked there for forty years in admissions, the longest of any one I know in our profession. He was dean of admissions at the time of his death. He and I traveled together many times to national, state, and regional conferences, as well as to many college day programs. I first met him at the high school in Marion, North Carolina his first week out on the road. He was one of my closest friends and I loved him. He and his wife, Eleanor, came to my house each Christmas for breakfast. Since his death, Wake Forest named the admission building 'The William Gray Starling' building.

Upon the death of Jean Rayburn in 1984, John Casteen, the former director of admissions and now president of the University of Virginia, had this to say about Jean at her memorial service: 'Jean came to the University in 1975 as Assistant Dean of Admissions and Assistant Professor in the General Faculty. She was educated at Queens College in Charlotte, North Carolina, the University of North Carolina at Chapel Hill, and Dartmouth College. Before coming here, she served as Director of Admissions at Queens College and at St. Andrews Presbyterian College in Laurinburg, North Carolina...Many of us remember her for her wit, which was both vast and apt. She knew the value of a story well told...To all of us, she gave moments of joyful understanding...Let us remember Jean for her generosity, her integrity, her commitment to quality and to equality, and her demonstration, living and dying, of the timeless values of good humor, good sense, and human compassion.' Further, Jean was the first non-UVA graduate, the first non-PhD, the first non-tenured professor, the first non-Virginian and the first woman to be appointed as director of admissions at the University of Virginia."

Over the years, these and the many other admission counselors and directors Charlie has gotten to know have been among his closest friends. Describing this group of professionals as a "fraternity," Charlie bonded with many each year during the fall recruiting period. Other counselors include:

Anna Kellar, Anne Collins, Anthony Locklear, Barbara Polk, Barry Bradberry, Ben Utley, Bill Fleming '73, Bill Mackie, Bob Gwaltney, Bob McLendon, Bob Newton '58, Bob Wicker, Bonnie Jones, Brona Roy (deceased), Bruce Stewart '61, Charles Lancaster, Charles Richard, Charlie Brock, Charmin Britt, Chris Kosiba '97, Chuck Edington, Chuck Rickard, Clay Alexander, Connelly Hilliard, Craig Fulton '73, Dave Warner, Ed French, Edith Kirkland, Edwin Wiles, Elaine Lyles, Emily Harper (deceased), Eppie Turner, Fannie Williams (deceased), Fran Jones, Fred Daniels, Glenn Hardesty, Grady Cathey, Grady Wicker, Jim Bundy, Jimmie Daniels, Joe Watts, John Bolin, John Cox (deceased), John White, Kathi Baucomb, Kathryn Knapp-Watts, Ken Raab (deceased), Malinda Richbourg, Margaret Perry, Margaret Rooke, Margaret Williamson, Marie Deans, Marion "Chubb" Richards, Pella Stokes '79, Peter Reichard, Randy Kilby (deceased), Ray Covington, Ray Strong, Richard Cashwell, Richard Thompson, Robert Barkley, Ross Griffith, Sara Bohn '78 Looman, Sayde Dunn, Shirley Hamrick, Stan Broadway, Steve Poston, Sue Kearney, Sue Sutton, Susie Aubuchon '79, Terry Davis, Tyree Kiser, and Wayne Bowery.

Additionally, Charlie has grown close to many high school guidance counselors in North Carolina through his travels, including: Sue Sutton, Lucille Browne, Melissa Thompson '72 Harrelson, Dorothy Miller, Nancy Marks, Judy Barrett, Helen Allison, Janie Weaver, Trudy Kastner, Nezzie Carter-Moore, Jane Lewis, Thelma C. Lennon, Jack Knox, Alice Solomon, Jean Leigh, Ella Stephens Barrett, Kathryn Ray, Betty Knox, Catherine Cutts, Mildred Simons, Irene Hankins, Glenda Poole, Alyce Sumrell, Jean Olive, Charlotte Cole, Janet Green, Ruth McSwain, Ethel Booth, Marie Deems, Joseph Champion, Chester Misenheimer, Louise Shelton, Richard Mock, Hildred Smitz, Virginia Daniels, Nancy Rowland, and Kate Parks Kitchen.

I THOUGHT HE HAD RETIRED!

When Grimsley Hobbs retired in 1980, Bill Rogers arrived from the northeast to replace him. "I met the Rogers and related to them very well right off the bat," Charlie recalls. One day a friend of the College's dropped by Founders Hall and asked Dr. Rogers how long it took him to realize how important Charlie was to the operation of the school. "About two weeks," was Dr. Rogers' response. "Had I known Bill Rogers had been there that soon, I might not have ever retired," Charlie admits. "His strength was in his relations to groups outside of Guilford. He was active in the Rotary, he was an outstanding speaker, and he sang in an opera here in Greensboro. Not only did he improve the quality of the student body, but he was well-known and respected in the community and in academia as well."

Beverly Rogers remembers those early years when her husband and Charlie got to know each other. "When Bill became president," she says, "the tables were turned and Charlie became the one chauffeured. It was not that Charlie liked driving less (he has been touring in his van all over the country), but Bill, who to this day loves cars and driving, was happy to whisk along in the college car while Charlie filled him in on history and geography and the comings and goings of all the college folks they were about to visit. Often I joined them on these trips. We all had a great time talking and teasing together."

It was during this time that Charlie got involved with the annual Guilford Choir Trip, at the bequest of the College's well-respected music director, the late Ed Lowe. Many years later, on one memorable choir trip through the southeast in March of 1993, the last concert was given in Atlanta at the beginning of a raging snowstorm. "By morning," Beverly laughs, "there was over a foot of snow on the ground, almost no plows working except at the airport, and the sparsest traffic on the highways that anyone in Georgia could remember. Bill, who grew up in the wintry Adirondack mountains of upstate New York, thought little of it, and set off to chauffeur Charlie and me back to Greensboro ahead of the choir bus. By our count, there were over one hundred cars and trucks scattered along in the ditches. People were either stuck or sliding as they tried to maneuver. Bill pressed steadily forward, and we soon arrived home safely and without incident. Afterwards, I suspected that Charlie had been a little scared, so I assured him that I had been praying for our safety. Charlie quickly retorted, 'I had a lot more faith in Bill's driving than in your prayer.'"

As it was, Charlie had begun to work out a retirement plan prior to Dr. Rogers' arrival. When retirement loomed at the conclusion of the 1983 academic year, Charlie began to look forward in earnest to his time away from campus. After all, he had spent several decades admitting, and then befriending, thousands of students. It was time for a break. When Guilford staff and administrators, along with other close friends, roasted him at a dinner at High Point Country Club that spring, Charlie was thrilled to learn that the college had begun fundraising efforts for the dedication of Hendricks Hall, which would continue to house the admissions office on campus.

However, contentment with some well-deserved rest and relaxation proved to be short lived. "I found I missed it a great deal, even during the first week," confesses Charlie. Guilford alumnus and friend Curt Hege had earlier agreed to lend him use of a beach house at Emerald Isle for an extended stay. Charlie moved there late in the summer of 1983, with plans to fish, catch some rays, and head up to Salter Path as he had with Esther and Ralph Cummings so many times to try a new flavor of ice cream.

While the easygoing lifestyle suited him for several days, boredom soon crept in and, as Charlie notes, "I ended up staying at the beach only two weeks even though I had intended to be there for four months. I was lonely and uninvolved."

When the Guilford admissions director at the time, Fran Cook, asked Charlie upon his move back to Greensboro if he would visit a few high schools, he jumped at the chance. He realized how much he had missed the admissions scene. "When I went to a few schools that fall and was talking to youngsters, I found I still got nervous and had a lump in my throat. Nothing topped admissions work. I had a renewed love for it." And now, nearly twenty years after his retirement, Charlie has spent between two and eight weeks every fall visiting high schools on behalf of Guilford.

A year later, in 1984, Hendricks Hall was officially dedicated. Beverly Rogers recalls, "In the 1980s, Guilford College renovated and expanded several major buildings on campus. In at least two cases, the field house and the library, these new facilities were named after major donors who helped substantially with the construction costs. Since the Continuing Education building was being remodeled to house both continuing education and undergraduate admissions, friends of Charlie raised sufficient funds to carry out their wish to name the building Hendricks Hall in honor of Charlie. Up until that time, no building on campus had ever been named in honor of a current employee, no matter how distinguished or loved." However the trustees, at the request of President Rogers, made an exception in this case. "It was one of the high points of my life," says Charlie. "It was a great honor considering I hadn't given much money and hadn't been an academic." Don Howie, who was living at Charlie's at the time, laughs at the memory of Charlie's dedication speech. "He proclaimed during his remarks that having a college building named after you proved three things—you don't have to be rich, you don't have to be smart, and you don't have to be dead." Those who were present that day will never forget those words.

In January of 1986, Charlie gave his friends and family a scare. A slight but increasing pain, which he believed to be indigestion, shot through his chest for more than a week. Finally, an emergency trip to the Wesley Long Hospital revealed something graver—a heart attack. After being placed in intensive care at Wesley Long, Charlie was transferred to Moses Cone, Greensboro's other renowned hospital, for an angioplasty. The operation was a success, and Charlie remained in intensive care for two weeks before moving to Friends Homes Guilford to recover for two months. A doctor performing a follow-up health check determined that the attack had been brought on by 'delayed stress,' a concept Charlie struggled with because, as he says, "I really hadn't felt stressed at all." Resolved to put himself into better shape, he began to walk the roads near his home five days out of every week, and by May of that year he had shed fifty pounds. At the age of sixty-seven, he had endured his first sojourn to a hospital.

Unfortunately, it would not be his last. In 1994, Charlie developed another pain, this time in his back. A few weeks after receiving a shot from his doctor, Charlie realized the pain was not subsiding. He decided to try another doctor. This time an MRI indicated a corroded disk that would need surgery. However, Charlie recovered from the surgery's effects in only one month, and he has been pain fee ever since. Charlie attributes his quick recovery in part to the support he received from his extended Guilford family. "All of my friends were very kind," he recalls. "The kindest act was when Jeff Kloss drove up from Atlanta and stayed with me before and after the surgery. It was like having family there."

Years earlier, in 1982, another family had formed around Charlie. A group of locals began to meet every morning for breakfast at a McDonalds on New Garden Road in Greensboro. For nearly four hours each dawn, the group would share jokes, advice, sympathy, and coffee before they headed their separate ways. Over the years the group has developed a tight-knit bond. Miss a day and someone will call and make sure that the person is in good health; if he or she is not, then papers will be picked up in the driveway by someone from the group. Four members of the McDonald's group had at one time or another been admitted to Guilford by Charlie—Peggy Wells Pope, David Barrow, Dick Pleasants, and Tommy White. Others who partake in the daily gathering include Peggy's husband

Graham, Charles Eichorn, Bobbie Bennett, Bonnie Ricketts, Betty Smith, Doug Henderson, Nancy and Joe Johnson, and Billie and Charles Gladwell. The McDonalds' staff of Clisanta Valverde, Mary Troxler, and Zack Cook has always taken such good care of the group that Charlie sends each of them a jar of his famous peanuts every Christmas.

Charlie has now been an active member of the college's alumni board since 1951, and in 1971 received the Distinguished Service Alumni Award from Guilford. (Somehow, he has also managed to find time to serve on the Board of Trustees at nearby New Garden Friends School). Though he does not travel to as many college fairs and high schools as he used to do, he still makes a point of advising young admission counselors who are new to the profession...even if they are work for other colleges or universities.

One such example is Clay Alexander. Clay recalls some advice he received a few years ago—"*Clay, if there is one person you need to get to know in order to be successful in admissions, it's Charlie Hendricks.*" He then made it a point to seek out Charlie while attending a conference in Greenville, South Carolina in December of 1996. "Our initial meeting was brief as we simply exchanged greetings, made small talk, and then went our separate ways," Clay notes. "I would cross paths with Charlie a couple of other times later that spring while recruiting in both eastern and western North Carolina. It wouldn't be until the fall of 1997, while sitting at my desk at Frances Marion University in Florence, South Carolina, that a phone call from Charlie would jump-start our friendship. During the conversation he wanted to compare travel plans for the upcoming months and then asked if I planned to recruit in North Carolina. Quite flattered that he called, I realized that one particular week of my schedule called for me to be in Fayetteville, as Charlie would be as well. He and I will always recall that particular week as the worst of the recruiting season but as the most fun we had all year. Over the next few years, Charlie and I traveled much of North Carolina together. We never missed an opportunity to eat a meal together, and if I was ever home visiting my family in Davie County, I was sure to head over to Charlie's. Soon new doors opened up for me. After three years at Francis Marion, I decided to head back to North Carolina and take a position at Catawba College in Salisbury.

Later, when I joined the admissions office at Greensboro College in September of 1998, I was living at home with my parents and commuting from Advance until I could find a place of my own in Greensboro. When Charlie learned that I was driving forty-five minutes one way to work he offered a room in his house in which to stay until I found a place of my own. Needless to say, I stayed seven months, moved to an apartment for three years, and have now moved back in with Charlie.

I've met more people in Charlie's living room than anywhere else. A real treat is getting to listen to stories of days gone by and of all the adventures he has experienced throughout his life. Charlie has lived so much of the history that I only learned about in high school and college. And his cooking! Charlie's hamburgers are by far my favorite. His homemade soup, baked peanuts, and applesauce are delicacies as well. If you truly know Charlie, you know that he is the most unselfish person around. One would think that he runs a rental car service considering how often he lets people drive off in his truck or van—so much so that sometimes he is without a vehicle to use himself. Even today, he is the busiest 'retired' human being I know. He'll admit to you that his calendar is more full now than it ever was before 1983.

A couple of years ago I went to Charlie for advice about a very difficult decision regarding my career. After three years in admissions at Greensboro College my former boss, now Vice President at Guilford, offered me a position in the admissions office at Charlie's alma mater. At the same time, Greensboro College was in the process of offering me the position in the President's office. Not knowing what decision was best, I consulted with my mentor. Charlie let me know that even though he would love for me to be a part of the Guilford experience, he realized the opportunity with Greensboro was one that I should not pass up. Receiving his honest advice helped me make the right decision. It is ironic, though, that if not for Charlie's advice I would still be in admissions, and I'd be at Guilford College."

Though he misses Bill and Bev Rogers greatly, the tenure of Gordon Soenksen in Institutional Advancement and the arrival of both Don McNemar and Kent John Chabotar as presidential successors has reminded Charlie why Guilford has such a permanent place in his heart. "Don and Britta and I got off to a good start in the first year they were here," he recalls. "That year the college choir sang its last concert of the spring tour in Wilmington, Ohio, Don's hometown. They and I drove from Wilmington to Guilford the last day. From the time we left Wilmington until we arrived at my home, we talked Guilford College all the way for eight hours. From that day on I felt very close to them. I introduced them to cheese grits, Fran's Front Porch, Hill-Billy HideAway and many other eating establishments. We went together to many alumni meetings, Friends meetings and to ball games. They added much to Guilford the time they were here."

Though Dr. Chabotar arrived at Guilford only in 2002, he is proud to be a part of the legacy of the connection between the school and Charlie. "I am the fifth of the five presidents of Guilford College for whom Charlie Hendricks has worked. There have been eight in total so that is quite an accomplishment," he admires. "His presence and contributions over many years were among the earliest things I learned upon arriving on campus. The expression 'been there, done that' applies to Charlie more than anyone else I've ever known in higher education. In fact, when Don and Britta McNemar hosted me for breakfast upon my appointment, the only other person at the table was Charlie—a true right of passage for new presidents.

About Charlie Hendricks, I have a variety of recent memories that typify the man and his service:

Charlie is a great cook. Not only has he had me over to his home for breakfast and lunch but also made me a peach cobbler to tide me over during my initial week at Guilford. It is not his fault that I still am not a big fan of grits, even the cheese grits that Charlie makes.

Charlie remembers. He hosted a fun party to commemorate the sixty-fifth anniversary of his class's matriculation at Guilford College in 1936.

He knows students and faculty and trustees over nine decades, and what they meant to him and vice versa.

Charlie stays involved. Charlie hosts informal get-togethers for athletes, raises money, hosts College staff at his home, and participates in an enormous number of alumni and other college events. It is strange for me to attend a college event—academic, social or athletic—and not have Charlie there.

Charlie is funny. First impressions might lead you to believe that Charlie is too serious, even gruff. No way. He has a dry sense of humor that allows him to tell a great story and to laugh heartily at the jokes of others. One time I noticed that he had photos in his home of every Guilford president except me, and teased him about it. Months later when I had forgotten all about it, Charlie put a postscript in a formal letter to me: 'I promise to get a picture of you on my mantel in the New Year.'

That's Charlie Hendricks."

During the past ten or fifteen years, Charlie has continued to promise his friends that he will slow down. "I'm not going to do much in the office this fall," one might hear him mumble before each academic year. However, his friends know that not a word of it is true! Charlie continues to put in long hours, whether through raising funds for college campaigns, attending college fairs, or urging alumni to return to campus for reunions. He still makes a concerted effort each year to get to know freshmen, and then make mental notes about their progress at Guilford over the next few years. Jeff Kloss, the student who lived at Charlie's for three years in the early 1990's, appreciates the efforts Charlie made when Jeff himself was an underclassman. "Charlie always claimed he did not want to mother me, but he did on a few occasions," Jeff recalls. "As many college students are, I was slack in my responsibilities. Charlie would always say, "Jeff, I don't want to be your mother, but…" He would remind me of appointments I had and other responsibilities I needed to complete. One time, I had overslept for a choir performance. We were to go to Chathem Friends Meeting for a concert. I had overslept and missed the bus! Ed Lowe came to the house to get me. I'm sure if Charlie had not been there, Ed would have made true on his threats he had previously made in jest in class. Once again, Charlie came to my rescue. Not only did he protect me from Ed's wrath, but he drove me to Chathem Friends in time for the pre-concert activities. I just happened to walk in when Ed was not looking, and took my place. Ed never said anything to me, but he sure gave me the evil eye. Charlie always said he didn't want to be my mother, but then he proceeded to act like my mother but being overly-protective and constantly looking after me. Now, on every Mother's Day I try to send Charlie a Mother's Day greeting card."

"One of my greatest treasures is the class ring Charlie gave me," Jeff continues. "As graduation was approaching, Charlie asked if I was going to get a class ring. I told him I would like to, but they cost too much money, and I was not one for jewelry anyhow. Close to graduation, Charlie pulled me aside and told me he had something he wanted to give me. He pulled out his silver class ring with a red stone and a silver scripted G engraved onto it. He said he would like for me to have it. Charlie had already opened his home and had given me so many things. Now he was offering me something so precious, beautiful and meaningful. That ring means so much more than just being a class marker. To me, it symbolizes our friendship and the dedication Charlie has toward Guilford College. Guilford to Charlie is not the brick and mortar that make up the buildings. It's not the many acres of land, it is not the trees, or open spaces, it is not even the degrees earned or the knowledge learned. It is the bond of friendship that he has developed over the fifty-plus years he has been at Guilford. Although there is fifty-two year difference from the date on the ring and the year I graduated, I would never trade that ring for another.

It has been ten years now since I graduated from Guilford, but I often come back to visit Charlie. I would visit with other friends and Charlie would always have several things he had scheduled for that particular weekend too. However, we would always make time for the two of us to eat and talk, two of Charlie's favorite activities. We would talk of things we were doing and of people we both knew. Charlie, always prefacing his advice with 'I not trying to be your mother, but…' It was always good advice. We would always sit on the sofa and continue our conversation. Soon the conversation would fade, and we would sit and commune in a language only true friends could understand. Charlie has taught me the meaning of true friendship. He has taught me what a selfless, loving, meaningful, connection should be. So many people's lives have been touched by this man. I am fortunate, for not only can I say that Charlie is my friend but that Charlie considers me his friend. He has never been wealthy, but he deals in a much richer currency, the warmth between people."

"I've really gotten to know Charlie in the past twenty years, after my husband, Ray Evans, died," says friend Mary Evans. "Ray used to own the hardware store near the college and he became friends with Charlie, Dr. Purdom, and Dr. Milner. I worked for Exxon in those days, so I didn't really know Charlie that well. But he has been a great friend. He is synonymous with Guilford College in my mind. He's just given his life to that school. Every Christmas, I bring him a box of sweet potatoes from down east. He eats one each day until they are gone. Charlie is a great Quaker, and he is mighty fun!"

Coach Jensen agrees. "One memory I have," Jack says "happened at a New Year's Eve party in the 1970's at our rental house on New Garden Road. We were playing 'Charades' and when it came time for Charlie's turn, he received his clue and began by getting down on the floor and rolling over and over—the sight of which caused everyone else to grow hysterical. After a few moments, and more rolling by Charlie, the wife of Coach Buzz Dunning, Barbara, yelled out, 'with six, you get egg roll!' As a result, Charlie's team won the game with that demonstration. It was hilarious and wonderful."

"Once, a few years ago, Don McNemar and Gordon Soenksen were taking me to the airport," remembers Monty Milner. "The flight got cancelled. So I asked Charlie "is there room in the inn?" He immediately cooked a meal for two, and there were leftovers. Earlier, I learned manual labor from Charlie—setting up chairs, etc. And his 75th birthday party was the easiest fundraising job I ever had. Furthermore, he was wonderful to my aunt and uncle as their health declined."

Susan Streitman Manz, wife of the college's chief financial officer, notes, "While I was not a Guilford student, Charlie and his admissions colleagues recruited my husband Phil to Guilford out of Roanoke Rapids High School in 1975. One of my favorite Charlie stories comes from his big birthday party in 1993. It was an absolutely perfect May afternoon and it was the day I met Charlie for the first time. It wasn't a typical day for Phil and me, but to be sure, a memorable one. And little did I know then that we would marry three and a half years later with Charlie playing a very important part of our wedding and our life."

Charlie also ushered at Bill and Pat Wearmouth's wedding. Bill met Pat during his days at Guilford, and maintained the relationship due in part to Charlie's generosity. "At the time," explains Bill, "I was dating my future wife, who was attending a South Carolina college south of Charlotte. 'Dating' is a stretch since I could barely afford a telephone call much less a trip to see her. I was cleaning the student union after closing hours to make what little money I had. Yet Charlie not only lent me his car, but he also included—at no charge to me—his gasoline credit card. So while I know how important he was to my courtship, my three children and nine grand-children will never be able to fully appreciate how they are indebted to him. And because of his generosity, a marriage did occur in August of 1960."

However, Charlie's ushering performance did not go as smoothly! Bill recalls that Charlie's duties "led to an embarrassing moment for him. Charlie was one of eight ushers and groomsmen at our wedding in a very large Episcopal church. They were all seated in the choir stalls at the front of the church, in full view of everyone during the communion portion of the service. Fortunately, I was kneeling at the alter rail and could not see this Quaker behind me vainly alternating between standing and kneeling in accordance with Episcopal liturgy. His fellow usher Groome Fulton can attest that this syncopated (compared with the congregation) 'rising and falling with the tide' could not have been better choreographed by the best Hollywood comedy director. As soon as he realized that they were up, he made his move, but only to see that they were going back down as he reached full height. So, to make things easier, he knelt as everyone else stood for the rest of the service."

In addition to the Manz and Wearmouth nuptials, Charlie has been a part of many other weddings. Among those were the ceremonies for the following:

Brad and Rhonda McIlwaine

Craig and Mona Fulton

Curt and Pat Hege

CW and Lena McCraw

Earl and Bettyjo Tyson

Gary and Sara Bowen

Groome and Anne Fulton

Hank and Kathy Cofield

Howard and Dorothy Gilbert Thorn

Jack and Ruby White

James and Gail Crumpler

James and Issie Morphis

Jeanne and Lefty Ralls

Jeff and Cherie Kloss

Jerry and Susan Rogers Howell

John and Ann Burwell

Linda and Van Cuthrell

Richard Haines and Martha Bell Edgerton

Robert and Beth Fulton

Robert and Nancy Newton

Winslow and Helen Womack

Mark Owczarski worked with Charlie for three years before returning to Syracuse, New York. Still, he has yet to meet or work with anyone quite like him. "Charlie Hendricks is one of a kind," boasts Mark. "He's among the few people I know who, by simple existence, create a common bond among total strangers. You could meet a total stranger on the street, and should you discover that each of you have been touched by Charlie, an instant bond of understanding is formed.

I'll never forget the first time I had a conversation with Charlie. In 1994 I had interviewed for the Director of College Relations position. I had met Charlie in the interview process, but really didn't speak with him at length. In spite of that, I knew from observing others that Charlie was a special person and someone I needed to get to know if I got the job. I ended up getting the position, and started at Guilford August 1, 1994, having moved south from New York. Shortly after starting, I decided that I'd head over to Charlie's house (he was home with a bad back) and introduce myself to him, try to get to know him, and start building a relationship with him. Kenneth Chandler, then director of Alumni Relations, walked me over to his house and helped with the introductions.

So after Kenneth's introduction, I started to babble on, 'It's so nice to meet you... it will be a pleasure working with you...I welcome your thoughts and ideas... I appreciate your help...' and so forth. To all of which, Charlie just looks at me, and in a way only Charlie can say it, deadpans, 'Last thing we need at Guilford is another damn Yankee. But let me know what I can do to help you.' Right then and there, after I got over my shock at his initial comment, I knew I would be working with someone special.

Working with Charlie was great. You always knew where you stood with him—one hundred percent honestly. If you messed up, (which I did more than once), he would tell you. But he wouldn't hold it against you. And as he did with generations of Guilford students and alumni, he would care about you as a person, too. He never lost sight of the fact that you, too, had feelings. And that life sometimes was hard, and what you really needed was a friend to help you get through it. Charlie Hendricks has been a great friend to me, and to thousands of other people. Maybe that's why many folks will say, 'Charlie...he's really a softie at heart.' That may be among the reasons that when Charlie walked into a room full of Guilford people, attention would inevitably turn to him. People of all ages, of all professions, of all backgrounds, would flock to him...to welcome him...to speak to him...to be with him. You could tell it was a respect that he cultivated over his entire life. And you could tell that people genuinely enjoyed being with him. I've never seen a person command such feelings from so many people in my life.

Even though I left Guilford in 1998, Charlie Hendricks remains a great friend to me. We talk all the time on the phone. The 'Hendricks Hilton' is always open to me when I pass through Greensboro. I won't leave town without sharing a meal with him. He's too special to me to pass up such an opportunity.

Charlie Hendricks is one of a kind. Guilford College is very blessed to call him his own. I am very proud to have been a part of Guilford College, and even prouder to have been able to share in Charlie's life. As the years have gone by since that time, I have learned even more how special Charlie Hendricks is and how important he is to the college. He has opened many doors during the 'Our Time in History' campaign. There is no telling how many appointments he has gotten for the various staff members by simply picking up the phone and calling a Guilfordian. His generosity is second to none. I have had the privilege of seeing him laugh and cry. I have seen his kindness and his gruffness and I have come to love him dearly, even though I have been just a new fresh kid in his long lifetime of friends, which is the true measure of his massive wealth. Charlie's friends are everywhere."

Dennis Haglan concurs with Mark. "During my second employ at Guilford, one of my most vivid memories was of Charlie and I traveling to visit the college's supporters," says Dennis. "He knew them all, and they all loved seeing him. One of the best trips we had came just before Christmas in 1999. I had scheduled a trip for us that would carry through seven states over four and a half days. Charlie was amazing for an 81 year-old. He would get up early, make our visits, travel to the next destination, and get to bed late—and at the conclusion of the trip he had much more energy than I. And he always seemed to know the correct directions to each location! Charlie's greatest love has always been Guilford College. He has given his life to the school, and at his death he will have given virtual-ly all of his possessions to it as well. It can truly be said of Charlie that 'he gave all he had.'"

Though Charlie has worked with many secretaries and assistants dur-ing his tenure at Guilford, his current stint in the Office of Institutional

Advancement has proven that while he and the technology of the 21st Century may not be a wedded couple, much can still be accomplished through simple cooperation and a roll-up-your-sleeves work ethic. (Charlie admits that computers have greatly improved office efficiency in comparison to 1952. "When I got my second secretary," he recalls, "I only had one typewriter, so the business manager brought me another one and said that the new typewriter was pretty good but that the 'A' did not always work. It was hard to use it as Director of Admissions and Financial Aid without an 'A.' It was soon corrected.")

Currently, Charlie is aided in his development work by Libby Rich and Helen Allen, two ladies who, in addition to other duties, type his hand-written letters, respond to email that may come for him, and fax important notes to alumni. Of course, while Charlie eventually grows to depend on each of his assistants, he brings every one of them along slowly. Libby claims that, "When I came to the advancement office five years ago, Charlie continued to call his previous secretary, Debbie Bowman, when he wanted something done. Cautiously, I started asking him if I could do some typing for him. After he realized that I really wanted to work with him, I was home free. I didn't know it, however, until I overheard him on campus one day tell someone that I indeed was his secretary. Charlie brings me flowers, applesauce, peanuts, potato salad, and cards on special occasions. Most importantly, he arrives at work with true friendship and caring." Helen agrees with Libby's assessment. "When I came to the office in 2000," she says, "Charlie would walk in and not even acknowledge that I was sitting at my desk. When he wanted something done, he would ask Libby. Eventually, the day came that Libby was out of the office and Charlie needed an address from our computer database...it was my golden opportunity! I eagerly dropped everything I was doing and found the information for him. And since that time, Charlie has called on me for assistance. Now when he comes into the office he greets me with 'good morning,' and he usually has some applesauce or flowers for me. He is a unique individual and great friend."

Other institutional advancement staff members have marveled at Charlie's continuing enthusiasm since 1992 in their department. Charlie Patterson, who has directed the office at the school for five years, recalls his first meeting with a chuckle. "I first met Charlie in May of 1998, so I am a relative newcomer to the wonderful world of Charlie. At that time, I was considering leaving Wake Forest University and coming to Guilford. My wife and I had dinner with our good friends, Dave and Lynn Odom, and Dave suggested that I ought to visit with Charlie, whom I did not know from Adam's house cat—can you imagine anybody in 1998 not knowing who Charlie Hendricks was? At any rate, Dave said, 'I will call and get you an appointment. When are you going for your interview?' I told him the date and time and then Dave called me the next day to let me know that I was having breakfast with Charlie at his house. At first I thought it was a little odd, but I now know that it is a common occurrence.

I drove from Winston-Salem to Greensboro and pulled into the driveway of the big white house on New Garden Road. There to greet me at eight in the morning was this jolly, old, elf-looking gentleman who served me warmed-over muffins with orange juice and who proceeded to tell me all the things wrong with the world, some of which belonged to Guilford College. I left Charlie's that morning a bit more confused but knowing that I had indeed been a guest of a very special man and, more importantly, I thought that I had him on my side as far as getting the job was concerned. I discovered later that it was not my knowledge of development or my personality that had won Charlie over, but in fact the simple reason that his friend, Dave Odom, had called on my behalf. That was all that Charlie needed to believe in me."

"My special time regarding Charlie was seeing the shy smile and the expression of fondness in his eyes when I presented him with his first teddy bear in September of 2002," remembers Neva Eckley. "It was my gift to him upon my sad departure from the Office of Institutional Advancement. Charlie made my job interesting to say the least. He'll always be in my thoughts and prayers. 'Miss America' is what Charlie, fondly, called me."

However, even those staff members who leave Guilford for other jobs or pursuits rarely go too long before being tracked down by Charlie. "Even though I eventually left Guilford to stay home," Esther Cummings says, "Charlie has remained a wonderful friend to my husband Ralph and me for many years. He has spent a week with our family at Emerald Isle every summer for over two decades. The fun, laughter, and nightly trips to Salter Path for ice cream have become tradition. Of course, another tradition is the one big disagreement he and I always have during the beach week. I have thought that he needed the advice of a 'wife,' and that I should be the chosen one. To my knowledge though, Charlie has never followed any of my suggestions!

Charlie's kitchen is a very special place. He gives the orders and we obey. For years he has served breakfast to members of the college choir before their departure at Spring Break. Once, as Ralph and I arrived to help, Charlie told me that I could cook the eggs—as high an honor as there is in his kitchen. I had been promoted after ten years of serving beverages!

Charlie is not a teacher, but he has taught our family so much. He has always been so interested in our children and grandchildren. 'Charlie is like my brother,' Ralph often says. We have been greatly enriched by his presence in our lives."

Like the Cummings family, Charlie's association with many families runs deep and can be traced directly to Guilford College in some manner or another. He has been particularly close to five North Carolina families. In their own words, the Fultons, the Gilmers, the Pleasants, the Ralls, and the Taylors have expressed what Charlie has meant to them throughout the years.

The Hendricks home in Archdale.

Charlie (top) and his brother Richard on the Hendricks farm in the 1920's.

In his dorm room in 1937.

Charlie receives his diploma in 1949.

At yet another college fair, this time in 1962.

Charlie (left) reflects on Guilford's 1973 national championship in basketball.

Looking sharp with Beverly Rogers in 1983.

Hendricks Hall

Charlie and college classmate, Seth Macon, at the Hendricks Hall cornerstone.

The Charles C. Hendricks Building Fund Donors

A distinguished group of individuals whose outstanding generosity demonstrates a commitment to the tradition of yesterday and the vision of tomorrow.

Robert W. Abrams
Edward H. '50 and Martha H. Alexander
Herbert and Ann Appenzeller
Jane H. Armfield
Susan M. Aubuchon '79
Richard and Linda Baddour
Howard H. Beaton '59
Karen '72 and Alfred A. Blum
J. James '62 and Marjorie S. Boles
Gary O. Jr. '57 and Susan E. Bowen
Mai Vu Brea '58
Reubene Brown
Kenneth W. Brown
Annie M. Brown
Christel Bullock
John B. Burns, III '66
Edward F. Burrows
Thomas L. Burton
Margaret Chalkley '56 and Stephen Webber
J. Howard Coble '53
Herbert H. Coffield
Hank Coffield
Carolyn R. Cogdell
Margaret Coltrane '37
Kenneth M. '70 and Vicky '70 Conrad
Stephen and Melva Cooper
Larry A. Jr. '52 and Patti '51 Crawford
E. Charles Cridlebaugh Jr.
William P. Danenburg '48
David M. Dickson '62
Ann '57 and Charles L. Echols, Jr.
J. Wilbert '40 and Marianna '40 Edgerton
James W. '66 and Karen English
Susan P. English '68
Carl O. '49 and Vivian Erickson
William M. B. Jr. '73 and Pamela '76 Fleming
William M. B. and Constance Fleming
Richard A. '53 and Sue Fletcher
Victor I. Jr. '52 and Rodgeryn Flow
Donald R. '64 and Yen Thi Foltz
Craig Fulton '73
Phillip D. '62 and Sandi Fulton
Robert D. Fulton '74
W. Groome Jr. '60 and Ann C. Fulton
Ruth Fulton
Diane L. Fulton '75
William S. Jr. '56 and Joyce '56 Gibson
Robert Gwaltney

Sara Elizabeth Hadley '44
Gordon E. Jr. '58 and Barbara '59 Haight
Jerry W. '72 and Melissa '72 Harrelson
Howard H. '57 and Patricia G. Haworth
John R. '47 and Martha W. Haworth
H. Curt Sr. '56 and Patricia '57 Hege
Charles C. Hendricks '40
James R. Hendricks '40
Vernera H. Hodgin
H. Paul '47 and Marie Jernigan
G. Henry Jr. '63 and Betty A. Jobe
Edward W. Jr. '63 and Linda '63 Kelly
Sol B. Jr. '49 and Eleanor D. Kennedy
Gene S. '51 and Polly Key
Katherine L. Knapp
Elizabeth '49 and Charles I. Kramer
Robert L. and Eleanor Krauss
Daniel F. Kuzma '64
W. Strupe '53 and Elizabeth Lackey
William T. Lauten Jr. '40
Sara J. '78 and John E. Looman
George W. Lyles III '69
Alan R. '64 and Molly A. R. Mabe
Miriam G. MacAllister '39
Cassie Mackie '49
James G. Mackie '50
Robert D. '59 and Judith G. '64 Marsh
Robert F. Marshall '51
James and Edith Mattocks
Charles R. Sr. and Edna McClellan
Charles B. McCurry
James W. McGinnis '42
William C. and Ruth McIlwain
James Bradley '79 and Rhonda McIlwain
Henry A. '68 and Carol '70 McKay
Charles F. Milner '33
Henry A. Jr. '57 and Helen Mitchell
Wilson Mitchell '40
Warren J. Mitofsky '57
James C. Newlin '60
James W. Newlin '41
Robert A. Newton '58
Warren C. '59 and Janet '59 Nichols
Hubert C. Jr. '65 and Lynn '67 Normile
Charles R. '65 and F Jane '62 Norwood
G. David '64 and M. Lynn '67 Odom
Elwood G. '64 and Ellen R. Parker
David R. Jr. '41 and Frances A. Parker

Mary Caulfield Parker '42
Mary Nell Parker '59
Keith E. Parks '69
David H. '66 and Bonnie Parsons
C. Owen '64 and Linda '65 Phillips
G. William III '65 and Clarajo '67 Pleasants
Herbert Poole
Patricia '58 and Frank H. Radey
Herbert T. '37 and Sharlia Ragan
N. Jean Ralls '49
George T. '50 and Patsy W. Ralls
Marion L. Ralls Jr. '48
Janice Reddick '68
James M. '65 and Ellen Reddick
Robert W. '71 and Judy '72 Rees
William R. and Beverley P. Rogers
Aileen Schoellkopf '49
Herbert J. Schoellkopf Jr. '48
Kenneth L. and Patricia Schwab
Herman W. Sexton Jr. '67
James L. Shelton '57
Wallace L. Sills Jr. '65
Bradshaw '48 and Ingeborg '49 Snipes
Ilet B. III '65 and Carol W. Southerland
David O. '44 and Helen '45 Stanfield
Bruce B. Stewart '61 and Andra Jurist
T. Eugene '49 and Eldora '49 Terrell
Manilius R. '69 and Elizabeth A. Thomas
Jack S. '55 and Helen '81 Thomas
E. Neal '69 and Amy K. Trogdon
John F. '67 and Doris '70 Van Etten
James M. Vogel '53
James E. III '65 and Elizabeth L. '64 Walmsley
Leslie E. Warrick Jr. '54
William H. '59 and Patricia Wearmouth
Charles A. Sr. '52 and Marilyn Whitcomb
Jack R. '40 and Ruby '40 White
Richard C. Whiteside '61
Ann E. Whitley '72
Samuel F. '78 and Amy Wishon
Juan Carlos '64 and Patricia Yarur
William L. Yates '53

Donors plaque for Hendricks Hall.

Speaking at the dedication of Hendricks Hall on May 5th, 1984.

Former Guilford President Don McNemar and his wife, Britta, get a laugh out of a Charlie story.

Still at work in the Office of Institutional Advancement in 2001.

Recruiting a future Guilfordian!

THE FULTON FAMILY

Charlie met the Fulton family at Quaker meetings in High Point. He also recruited the brothers to Guilford from high school.

Craig Fulton: "Recently I attended a SACAC meeting in Atlanta. We had signed on with a company's new software-recruiting package. As a result, the company had been telling everyone that they had UNC-Charlotte as a charter client. All during the SACAC meeting people were approaching me and saying that if Craig Fulton and UNC-Charlotte are doing it, it must be the real thing. It gave me a warm feeling to be a respected innovator in our field. I would not be that individual were it not for Charlie and had I not modeled my career after his. He taught me to treat individuals in our business with dignity and respect, the importance of admissions as a public relations position, of building a resume based on character and honesty. And he taught me how to have fun doing it. As a result, I have risen to a position of dignity and respect myself.

Our personal relationship is even more important to me than our professional one. I have always been closer to him than I have been to some family members. He always gave me understanding and 'room' to grow up. He never judged my poor decisions. In fact, during those times, he encouraged me most. He gave me a chance and encouraged me to finish college. He gave me a home to live in when I wanted one, not that I needed one. How many times have I spent in his house or his barn apartment?

Charlie's door has always been open to me, and it's always been my first choice of places to visit and stay. I've never felt unwelcome there.

As I think back, a key point in my life came when Charlie suggested me for a position on Guilford's alumni board. From that point on, I became seriously interested in admissions. Shortly, he guided me and supported me as I left Groome's business and joined the staff at Guilford, which proved to be one of the happiest days of my life. I am sure he can remember all those talks with Fleming, Pella, Poole, McIlwain, Sarah Bohn, and Robert Fulton.

Charlie, you have always helped me keep in touch with my spirituality. The Quaker influence and emphasis on values that Quakers hold constant continue to guide me in my daily life. There can be no better path along life's road than the consensus building and tolerance taught to us in the Queries of Quakerism. I think of this, and you, often."

Groome Fulton: "Where do you begin when reviewing a lifelong friendship? I first met Charlie Hendricks at Lake Singletary, near White Lake, while attending a Quaker summer camp. This was before the North Carolina Yearly Meeting developed Quaker Lake in the late 1940's, so I was about ten years old at the time. Charlie was the 'chief cook' and we—the campers—were the 'bottle washers.' My memories of Charlie center on good fun, wholesome fellowship, and of course, good food. Those three ingredients have always been present in any Charlie-related activity. Whether the gathering is a Guilford basketball game, a delicious breakfast at his house, a late night trip to the old dairy bar at Friendly Shopping Center, and alumni board meeting, Quaker Club activity, or just a plain old assortment of friends, you can count on fun, fellowship, and food. The Fulton Family has been intertwined with Charlie in so many aspects of our lives. From Camp Singletary and later Quaker Lake, to yearly meetings, to the trip to Kansas City in 1973 for the NAIA basketball championship, to all three of his retirement celebrations, to his annual Christmas Day visits to our family gatherings. We may go some time and not speak or visit, but when we do run into him, it is always as if we were never apart. We pick up

immediately where we left off because of the genuine, deep sense of friendship. Charlie's advice and counsel to various members of our family have
been invaluable. He is sometimes subtle but most often is very direct. He has
always been available for help if needed. I have particularly enjoyed observing the interaction between Charlie and new members to our family. Wives,
daughters, and sons-in-law warm to him so quickly.

Phillip Fulton: "I have known Charlie Hendricks for quite a few years
now. It seems that we have a lot in common. My first recollection of
Charlie is from Quaker Lake Camp, where he was cooking, and one of my
favorite pastimes is eating. In Charlie's dining hall we not only ate but
drew assignments out of a jar which gave us tasks, such as setting the table,
serving, cleaning up, washing, drying, or putting away dishes for our table.
When I dine at his table now, I am not required to do any of these tasks,
but I would gladly do them just to get my legs under his table more often.
His culinary talents are legend and I'm always fascinated with the utensils
he uses—beautiful blue and white enamel pans, blue and white sponge-
ware bowls, yellowware deep dishes and bakers—all valuable collectables
or antiques that most people would hang on the wall or use only for dec-
oration. Charlie actually cooks in them.

Charlie and I share a love of antiques. Some people think *he* is an
antique. I don't know about that, but he is probably older than most
items found in antique shops today. His house looks like a shop, and I
understand that at times people used to see his porch loaded up with
stuff, stop, ring his doorbell, and ask "what time does your shop open?"
The porch is neater now and most of the treasures have been removed to
his attic. But I love people who save things, and Charlie and I are certainly
birthright members of that group. I think Quakers are generally known
for keeping stuff. Every item has a little story and I like to remember
where things came from, and who owned them, and then imagine what
times were like back then. It's a little like having the folks still with you.
And I never look at my front door without thinking of Charlie. It was
once the door into Founders Hall on campus at Guilford, probably

installed around 1900. It was taken out of service during one of the many renovations, saved of course by Charlie, and given to Sandi and me when we built our house in 1974. Quakers recycle!

Charlie got a head start on me collecting, but since 1982 I have made a very good effort to catch up with him. This brings me to a story. Once, I was telling Charlie about all the good little shops up around Galax, Virginia where I traveled in my business. I would hit a couple places on the way up, take my customer to lunch, then stop at a few more shops on the way back. A man can only do so much in one day! Well, Charlie naturally was chomping at the bit to go with me one day. We rode up Highway 52 through Fancy Gap and made our first stop near Hillsville. I told Charlie that this guy gets in some nice things, but his prices are too high to buy anything. So I just stop in to sharpen my eye and see if there might be a bargain. Charlie promptly bought three old pocket watches and some other stuff and I knew right then that Charlie wasn't along just for the ride. We made a couple of other stops and Charlie wasn't bashful at those either, and I figured if we got overloaded, I could always pick up some things on my next trip. I later started traveling in a van. I dropped Charlie off at a little shop in Galax owned by Glenn and Cora Cole while I made my sales call. When I returned, they had become fast friends and there was a stack of quilts, quilt tops, old pictures, and several old mixing bowls to add to our cache.

The next stop in Galax was a shop owned by an old boy who refinished furniture and restored old stoves. He had restored an old wood stove of blue porcelain and chrome that was a beauty. Charlie wanted that thing badly. I could imagine it in his kitchen with candied yams and a big pot of black-eyed peas simmering on top and a big pan of biscuits inside, and me sitting at the table ready to chow down. The only thing that kept him from buying it was that he already had two! And for years afterwards, he asked me about that stove. I later bought a Wythe County pie safe from that dealer in Galax. He had just gotten out of a hen house and wanted to sell it quickly before his wife saw it and made him refinish it. It was pretty rough. He hid it for me until I could borrow Charlie's truck to pick it up.

When Charlie saw it, he asked 'did you really pay money for that?' I answered 'yes, and it will clean up nice too.' Charlie likes primitives, but I could tell that it was a little too primitive for him. Down the hill we came on Highway 89 through Sparta, Glade Valley, Doughton, and State Road, and at each stop we added to our plunder. I don't remember if I bought much or not, but I was enjoying watching Charlie work, and of course, my car would only hold so much.

Our last stop was near Elkin, North Carolina, at a 'group shop,' or mall as it is now known. We split up to cover the shop before closing time just as Charlie spotted some 'moss rose' pattern china, which he still collects today. When I came back around, he had a big stack of plates, cups and saucers, bowls, cream and sugars, and I heard him ask if any of the other dealers had any more. Well, he and the owner started searching the bottoms of cupboards, under tables, and inside of boxes and came up with considerably more. Charlie bought it all! We had a great day. The economy of that area got a pretty good boost that day. I continued to work Galax for several more years, and whenever I stopped in those shops everyone would ask about Charlie and when I was going to bring him back—and I think they would have been willing to chip in for the gas money if I did!"

THE GILMER FAMILY

Charlie has known the Gilmer family for forty years.

Charlie: "I met Douglas Gilmer when he first came to work at
Guilford College on January 16, 1963. He was hired to work for the dining service when John Lee was the manager. Since that time he has done
many things, not only for the dining service but for the College as well.
He has helped more students than anyone I know and he personally
knows as many Guilford graduates as I know. More importantly, he has
their respect.

There is nothing that I would not do for Douglas, and there is nothing that he would not do for me. If anything breaks down at my house, I
call him. If I have trouble with my car, I call him. If I need someone to
give me a ride to the doctor or the airport, I call him. In return for this,
he is the only person I would let borrow my new van to drive to Buffalo
in 1999 and to Atlanta on several other occasions. We have not kept
track, but I am sure that he has done more for me than I have for him.

About thirty years ago, I was looking for someone to help me keep
my house in order, and Doug suggested that his mother could do the
job. Those who know me and have seen my house know what a job that
must be. Well, she not only worked for me and did a great job, but she
also became my friend. Her name was D. A. Gilmer, but I always called
her 'Mrs. Gilmer,' even though her other friends and family called her

'Sug.' What a wonderful person she was! Mrs. Gilmer was a leader in the community and her church. She loved sports and did not miss many Atlanta Braves games on television. As the matriarch of seven boys and seven girls, thirty-two grandchildren and thirty-eight great-grandchildren, her home was always open for family and guests.

During the time that Mrs. Gilmer worked for me in my home, she did not miss a single day unless there was snow or ice on the ground. She simply did not set foot outside her door if there was a flake anywhere in the area. She always arrived at eight o'clock and stayed until she finished, even using her own key for entry if I was not in town. We never had a cross word between us during our thirty years of friendship. Like Douglas, she was a hard worker. Some years back, my friend Monty Milner remarked, 'I hope Ms. Gilmer will work at Charlie's forever, because no one else will be able to clean those antiques!' She worked for me until several years ago when her daughter, Marcy Wright, took her place and also became my friend.

Mrs. Gilmer died on October 19, 2002. I was honored to be asked to speak at her memorial service. My remarks ended thusly: 'I know for sure that Mrs. Gilmer is up in Heaven, sitting at the right hand of God. In fact, I know that when she met her Master, He quoted Proverbs 31— *Her children arise and call her blessed. Many women do noble things, but she surpassed them all.*'

Without a doubt, the Gilmer family has been an important part of my life for the past forty years and continues to be."

THE PLEASANTS FAMILY

Charlie recruited Bill and Clarajo Pleasants out of high school in the early 1960s—Bill from Garner and Clarajo from Asheboro.

Clarajo Pleasants: "Charlie never had a wife or any children. At eighty-four, he says it's not too late if he could just find someone with whom he wanted to spend that much time. However, does have an enormous 'adopted' family filled with scores of his contemporaries, friends, and their children, many who choose to call him 'Uncle Charlie.' One such relationship is with Bill and Clarajo Pleasants and our children. In their younger years, the Pleasants children, Clarke, Jim, and Lane, frequently asked, 'Now, just how is it that we are related to Charlie?' It was hard for them to believe that someone could be such an important part of their lives and *not* be a relative.

The Pleasants family has known Charlie for the greater part of fifty years—I knew Charlie during childhood years at Quaker Lake and Asheboro Friends Meeting, and both Bill and I as students at Guilford College (classes of 1965 and 1967, respectively). Immediately after graduation, when Charlie was head resident of English Hall, Bill spent weekends in Charlie's apartment when he came back to campus to see me. In fact, Charlie was later instrumental in hiring Bill at Friends Homes as Executive Director, saying, 'That was one of the best day's work I ever did.'

Actually, the Pleasants' fondest memories of Charlie developed after 1977 when they moved into Arcadia on the Friends Homes campus and subsequently acquired him as a neighbor. Charlie became a regular visitor several times each week, stopping by on his way home from work and joining the family for meals (if he liked what I was cooking). For quite some time, I thought that he didn't like either women *or* children and that he probably just came by to see Bill; however, I soon noticed that Charlie began to stop by just to see me even when Bill was not at home. I also observed that he obviously *did* like children because he spent lots of time with the boys and frequently could be found rocking Lane in the big plaid chair in the den trying to teach her to say 'Uncle Charlie.'

Bill and Charlie spent numerous hours going to antique auctions and refinishing furniture in Bill's workshop. One was working, the other talking, but they always made a good team. Bill remembers one occasion when he and Charlie were returning from Axton, Virginia in the old blue Ford truck with so much furniture loaded in the back that it had to be strapped in several directions just to keep the things from falling off. As luck would have it, the truck broke down and a patrolman rolled in behind them. Bill advised Charlie, 'Just keep cool and don't say anything.' Charlie's hands were shaking and he was biting his lip to keep from speaking. The patrolman left the guys on the side of the road but returned a short time later with a mechanic who there on the spot fixed the truck so these two 'oakies' could get home that night. Can you imagine what must have been going through the minds of that patrolman and mechanic?

The duo made other trips together, one of which was to solicit funds for the Regan-Brown Field House at Guilford. One time, the trip had not been particularly successful since they had asked the alum for a $30,000 contribution and he had responded, 'Well, I guess I could give $300.' To end the day on a happier note, Charlie convinced Bill to stop on their way home at his mountain cabin located at the foot of Buffalo Mountain near Willis, Virginia. All would have been fine except Charlie forgot to mention that the road ceased to exist about half way up the mountain. One other minor detail—there had been an ice and snowstorm the day before.

Undaunted, this fearless twosome left the main road and proceeded up the mountain road until the car wheels began to spin on the ice. When the vehicle began to slip backwards, Charlie, who was driving, opened his door in order to see better as he attempted to steer. With all the poise of a ballet dancer, the car slipped gracefully down the hill and rammed the open door into an embankment. The car could not move forward because of the ice and it would not go backward because the door was wedged. It was getting late and cold, so a plan was devised: *Charlie, the heavier of the two, was supposed to sit on the front fender opposite the stuck door. Hopefully his weight would lower one side of the car thereby raising the other side, and dislodging the door. Bill's job was to sit inside the car and pull the door shut once it was freed.*

The plan might have worked had not Bill looked up to observe this bulk of a man in a red toboggan bouncing on the front fender. The angrier Charlie became, the faster and higher he bounced... and the more he bounced, the harder Bill laughed... and the more Bill laughed, the angrier Charlie became.

Bill, by now, was laughing so hard that he was crying, and Charlie had resorted to four-letter words (Quaker ones, of course). Somehow amidst this hilarious scene, the door worked itself free enabling this 'odd couple' to proceed home without getting to the cabin and with Charlie refusing to speak with Bill. Even to this day, one man finds humor in the story and one man does not!

The Pleasants have spent a lot of their time with Charlie purchasing, hauling, or moving antiques. In fact, between trips to purchase antiques and move Charlie from one house to another, not to mention shuffling his inherited furniture, Bill, the boys, and I (with the help of Douglas Gilmer) have probably moved every piece of furniture of Charlie's at least three times. But Charlie is always generous in taking great pleasure in sharing his beautiful china and antique furniture collections. He has been known to end a moving or antiquing day by saying, 'I have just the thing to go on your shelf or in that corner.' The Pleasants home has many pieces of blue willow china and special antiques that Charlie has given to them with these words, 'I want it to have a good home, for after all you are my family.' Then with some hesitation, 'Of course, I may want it back sometime.'

In retrospect, the best part about being Charlie's neighbor was the relationship that developed between him and the three Pleasants children. Lane was just a toddler when she learned to watch at the window for Charlie's red van (or 'stran' as she called it) and Clarke and Jim took pride in washing it for him. Both Bill and Charlie enjoy harassing me about an event that occurred during one of these van-washing sessions. I had to leave and was preparing to ease my car past the van to exit the driveway. The boys moved all the washing supplies and bucket to the side of the drive only to see their mother run right over all the materials with the car. Without missing a beat, Charlie proclaimed, 'And they want to be equal!' Bill, Charlie, and the boys still love telling this story, and I, speaking for all women, still remind Charlie that he has not been forgiven for such a remark.

Charlie's vehicle also provided other great memories for the Pleasants. For approximately twenty summers, the family piled into the van with Charlie to head off to Topsail Beach. During the process of building the Pleasants' beach cottage, the van made numerous trips full of building supplies, cross ties, and kitchen cabinets. In fact, the wainscoting in the great room came from barn siding at Charlie's home place near Archdale. Charlie still contends that he wouldn't have a back problem today if it hadn't been for unloading the van and lugging cabinets up the steps while the cottage was being built.

One memorable afternoon at the beach, Charlie took charge of Lane who was about four years old at the time. He found that she had acquired at least a ton of sand in her bathing suit. He promptly took her to the cottage, gave her a bath, and prepared her for a nap. Lane made it clear she would not sleep unless Charlie took a nap too, which really didn't take much persuasion. So, they both piled into bed and vied for the title of 'loudest snorer.' Charlie later confessed it was the first time he'd ever bathed a girl and then gone to bed with her. Hmmmmmm!

Lane loved to visit Charlie's house on Arcadia all by herself and did so frequently when Charlie would stop by after work to take her home to play with his dog, Tig. On one occasion, Lane had not been a 'star rester' at kindergarten and had subsequently received a note from the teacher. So mother Clarajo told her she could not go to Charlie's house that afternoon and that Lane would have to be the one to tell Charlie why. I excused myself while Lane tearfully explained to Charlie why she could not go. This big man leaned down to Lane and said (tearfully too, it appeared) to her, 'Don't worry, I still love you.' He later reprimanded me in a huff with these words, 'Well, hell! It's not like she was smoking marijuana!' He then stormed off to his house.

Charlie never missed a birthday for any of the family and always orchestrated some kind of meal and a special gift. Sometimes he would plan a big gathering for the birthday party or a trip to a favorite restaurant chosen by the birthday boy or girl. On occasion, Charlie would sometimes even take the respective Pleasants sibling to a store to pick out a gift. For many years when Lane was in elementary school, Charlie would take her shopping for school supplies. This particular tradition made the family think he was making up for all those years when his own school supplies were pretty limited.

Charlie's relationship with the Pleasants boys was cemented by the fact that he never missed a single one of their home football games or for that matter other events in which they participated. When Jim, the younger of the two, played his last game, Bill and the two boys presented Charlie with a trophy that read, 'The 12th Man Award to Charlie Hendricks in appreciation for never missing a single one of our games.' During Jim's years at the University of North Carolina, Charlie made it a practice to go to Chapel Hill once a week to take him to lunch or dinner under the pretense that he was there visiting Richard Hendricks, his brother. Bill and I knew this and appreciated that he was checking to make sure Jim was okay, something that parents couldn't do as openly as Charlie could. And of course, nothing would do but that Charlie fly to Colorado to see Clarke graduate from the Air Force Academy. Though this turned out to mean sitting through the entire event in the rain, Charlie never considered missing a minute of it. What dedication!

Charlie's commitment to the boys and Lane also was evidenced by his preparing a midnight breakfast for them, their dates, and friends on their respective prom nights. When Clarke got married, Charlie hosted a bridal breakfast the morning following the wedding that actually sparked a rumor that Charlie had died. In keeping with the wedding festivities, he had hung a garland of ivy and white ribbon on his door. The neighbors and several friends naturally assumed that Charlie had passed, and one actually called the funeral parlor to see if the body had arrived. The undertaker replied, 'not yet.' Charlie loved every moment of this mix-up and will still be laughing outrageously when the next white wreath is hung on his door.

Some relationships are perfect with everyone living happily ever after. It was not to be so for Charlie and the Pleasants. The little blonde-haired girl, named Lane, who adored Charlie and was the only one in his life who could actually call him 'Chuck' to his face and boss him around, lost her life at the age of twenty-one following a lung transplant to fight the disease, cystic fibrosis. Charlie never wanted to discuss her illness; at the same time, he never failed to bring her flowers or a surprise when she was sick or hospitalized. Even after her death, he found ways to comfort the Pleasants family and seemed to find pleasure in donating to the scholarship established in her name. His last act of kindness for Lane came when he donated a dozen red roses, placed in one of his big blue vases, to her church when the scholarship in Lane's name was awarded. The note in the church bulletin that day read, 'From Uncle Charlie, a close friend.'

What more needs to be said? The Pleasants and Charlie... Close friends! Family!

THE RALLS FAMILY

Charlie became best friends with Lefty Ralls in 1947 when Lefty was a Guilford sophomore and Charlie had returned to campus. He had met Lefty's brother Jace two years earlier, and would also later meet Lefty's brother Bob.

Bob Ralls: "I was the third Ralls to attend Guilford College, following in the footsteps of my brothers Lefty and Jace, so I was fortunate in already knowing Charlie when I enrolled as a freshman. As I got to know him personally through my own relationships, he was always 'Charlie the Encourager.' I have never known anyone to take a more personal interest in so many. I happen to be one of his hundreds of very close friends!

Charlie meant the most to me when I switched majors and became a pre-ministerial student during my junior year. Immediately he invited me to start participating in some challenging Deputation Teams, which visited Quaker churches across the Yearly Meeting. He let me 'cut my homiletical teeth' on the Quakers. The beautiful Marilyn Lynhart would sing 'I Walked Today Where Jesus Walked,' and I would preach. Far more than giving me a chance to practice preaching, Charlie was always an encouraging voice. He even let me run my sermon ideas by him.

Later, when I attended graduate school at Duke and at Edinburgh and then had my own church, I never found myself too surprised to look up and see good 'ole Charlie sitting out there checking up on me and giving nods of encouragement. Even today, every time I encounter Charlie he invariably inquires about my wife, Aileen, and our two sons Mark and Scott, as well as their own families. When Mark became a minister himself, Charlie drove to hear him preach just as soon as he could. When Scott recently became a college president, Charlie showed up at his office, and out of his wisdom and experience, made Scott feel mighty good about himself. I really don't know how Charlie does it, how he makes the time to encourage so many! The Ralls clan looks upon Charlie Hendricks as a member of the family."

Jace Ralls: "Who could have possibly imagined that a chance meeting with a Conscientious Objector in 1945 at a Greyhound Bus Station in Washington, DC would be the beginning of a lifelong friendship? At the time I was stationed at the Bainbridge Naval Base in Maryland and Charlie was in the C.O. camp at Mount Weather. We were both with mutual friends from Greensboro who were meeting in Washington for a weekend of R&R. I remember thinking during that weekend, *what a strange guy Charlie is to support his country in such a passive way.* However, I learned that he was a very special person who cared a lot for his friends and country, and he introduced me to a new way of relationships. While reading *The Greatest Generation,* a book about World War II heroes and heroines, I thought that there ought to be a chapter about Charlie or about people like Charlie who encouraged us to solve problems in a peaceful manner and build positive relationships. I realized then that philosophy was what he was all about.

I had no idea that I would ever see Charlie again, but after I arrived at Guilford in 1946 there he was, as big as life, laughing and talking to students as they snacked and met for dates at the campus soda shop (which at the time was affectionately known as 'Charlie's Bar'). He built relationships as he managed this beehive of campus activity. Further, he managed the wait staff in the dining hall, and within a short time I found myself working on the staff and being one of his close friends. What I further learned about him was that whenever something important was happening or whenever someone needed a friend or money or a car, Charlie was there. If you wanted to be around good people, you stayed close to him.

As a member of Guilford's basketball and baseball teams, I remember Charlie's great interest in athletics. I don't believe he missed many games during my four years. He was always visible after contests, win or lose, congratulating or consoling my teammates and me. Charlie has probably attended more Guilford athletic events than any other person. It was because of his great love and support for Quaker sports that he was selected as a member of the school's Athletic Hall of Fame and as a life member of the Quaker Club Board. One of his finest hours occurred when he and my brother Lefty celebrated Guilford's 1973 championship in Kansas City. Lefty was President of the Quaker Club at the time and his son John played on the team. A victory celebration was held at Jefferson Standard Country Club where Lefty presided and Charlie served as Master of Ceremonies.

Charlie has continually kept a Guilford presence fresh in my life as we have celebrated birthdays, weddings, births, and retirements, and we have held each other in the light as we experienced the deaths of close family and friends. One of my prized possessions from Charlie is a pair of antique prints and picture frames that he loaned to Pat and me when we married fifty years ago. I think he finally gave them to us on our twenty-fifth wedding anniversary. Not only is Charlie a great friend to the three Ralls brothers, but he is also a special friend to our entire family. Eighteen members of the Ralls family attended his seventy-fifth birthday party in 1993.

Three annual events that stand out in my mind with Charlie include fishing excursions to Morehead City with him, Lefty, Ed Alexander, and Winslow Womack, trips to the Dixie Classic basketball tournament, and frog-gigging ventures to Quaker Lake. I recall our first trip to Morehead City quite well because the captain of our boat accused Charlie of pulling his line in so slowly that he was drowning his fish. Our most memorable Dixie Classic event occurred when we saw powerful Cincinnati, with the great Oscar Robertson, lose two out of three games to 'Tobacco Road' teams. As for the frog legs, they proved to be delicious to eat, but they were acquired with some risk, as we went along uneven lake banks at night and often encountered snakes that were searching for the very same prey.

In 1978, Charlie called to see if I would assist Guilford in completing a fund raising campaign for the new field house. I agreed to do so, and he and I made many calls on alumni asking for financial support. It was during that time that I realized again that what Charlie was really doing was building relationships for the college. After renewing old friendships, reliving Guilford memories, and putting the needs of the school in proper focus, the monetary 'ask' came quite naturally.

After a successful completion of that event, I became a full-time staff member of Guilford's Development Office. During the next ten years, Charlie and I worked closely on a number of projects. He was a great friend but an even better co-worker. Together, we did some important work for Guilford College.

In the fourteen years since my retirement from Guilford, we continue to see each other regularly as we both serve as life members on the school's Alumni Board and Quaker Club Board. We attend many ballgames together. It appears that our friendship will be intact for several more years because we have both signed up to live in Friends Homes Guilford in the not too distant future. A relationship that began in a bus station fifty-eight years ago is destined to continue!"

Jean Ralls: "Charlie is a unique individual—there is no one else like him. He has been a special friend to so many people. It would be interesting to know how many weddings he has participated in and how many children have been named in his honor—I can claim one of each.

In 1959, my husband, Lefty Ralls, and I moved with four children (number five came later) to Charlie's neighborhood. For the first few years he, along with other neighbors, came to our house very early on Christmas mornings to watch the children open their gifts. Afterwards, we all headed over to Charlie's house for breakfast. As the children grew, we continued to gather there. We are still meeting at his house on Christmas Day, and my family and Charlie are the only ones from the original group. Thirty or so friends drop by for his country ham, sausage, bacon, eggs, biscuits, fruit cup, fresh squeezed orange juice, coffee, and lots of fellowship. This is a tradition we all look forward to each year."

THE TAYLOR FAMILY

Charlie got to know each of the Taylor children through college fairs conducted at Pilot Mountain High School.

Anne Taylor Frost: "In the spring of 1957 Miss Willie Lou McGee, the math teacher at Pilot Mountain High School, took me to 'May Day' at Guilford College. That visit sealed the deal. In the fall I enrolled at Guilford and spent the next four years working for Charlie in the admissions office (for the amazing sum of fifty cents an hour). Charlie was a good friend; he gave me lots of advice—'don't come into Memorial Hall with Bermuda shorts on!'—and took my friends and me on 'recruiting' visits on Sundays to Quaker Meetings in nearby counties where we shared in the worship and got a good Sunday dinner.

During my four years at Guilford, Charlie (often accompanied by Professor Ed Burrows and some of my classmates) visited our home in Pilot Mountain. I know Charlie must recall one May when my mother made a birthday cake for him. After I graduated and my younger brothers carried on the Guilford tradition, the bonds between our family and Charlie deepened. My parents enjoyed camping and would often camp at the home Charlie and Richard owned near the Blue Ridge Parkway. They certainly remember Charlie's hospitality and all the fun they had there.

Charlie hosted parties for us when my brothers Tom and Steve graduated. It was at Steve's party that a discussion developed between Charlie

and his next-door neighbor, Ed Burrows, about the kudzu that was grow-
ing over on to Ed's property. After listening to Ed's complaints, Charlie
finally retorted, 'At least the kudzu doesn't make any noise!' Over the
years, Charlie has been part of the important events of the entire Taylor
family. From 1961, when my husband Miles Frost and I were married in
Pilot Mountain, to 2000, when Sarah Love Taylor, my niece, graduated
from Salem Academy, Charlie has been a big part of our family celebrations. He has attended our weddings, anniversary celebrations, graduations, and our children's weddings. We recall inviting him to Christmas
dinner once years ago, and he told my mother, 'I've got four other invitations, but I'm coming to your house.' He did... arriving with a pot of
homemade applesauce in a blue enameled pot.

To this day, if Charlie calls Steve or me and says, 'Meet me for lunch; I
need to talk to you about something,' you can bet we'll be there!

Tom Taylor: "My first memories of Charlie are tied to Anne's first years
at Guilford. Every time I saw him at Guilford or Pilot Mountain while
Anne was in college, Charlie always asked if I was coming to Guilford.
Although I was considering other schools, his personal interest in me and
my future was heart-warming; besides, I knew that I would never hear the
end of it from him if I went elsewhere. Moreover, he represented the same
fine qualities that I admired in Miles Frost (who married Anne) and their
other friends—such as Allen and Betty Lou Atwell, Tom and Lillian
O'Briant—good people who cared about others and wanted their lives to
make a difference.

Once at Guilford, I knew that I could count on Charlie for a friendly
welcome and helpful encouragement and advice, usually unsolicited but
always appreciated. I remember his sitting with me in the old Student
Union (now most appropriately named Hendricks Hall) my sophomore
year and telling me it was more important to get a good education and
make good grades than to be trendy or popular. He then reeled off the
names of Guilford alumni who had been successful scholars, professionals,
and—by the way—contributors! He also passed on a lot of social advice,
including ongoing critiques of practically every Guilford co-ed that I ever

dated, including Susan Belk, to whom I have been married for thirty-five years now. Without getting too specific, Charlie would let me know that this or that girl was better for me than the other, and why. For example, he volunteered one time that a particular co-ed seemed too negative in her attitudes toward Guilford, which automatically made Charlie suspicious. What would I have done without him? Although I was never sure that Charlie completely approved of my lifelong affiliation with the military as an officer and civilian lawyer, he has always been interested in what I was doing and supportive of my career. Whenever we have a chance to talk, it is as if we had just seen each other in the last few days, instead of years."

Steve Taylor: "Charlie was more of a fixture by the time I attended Guilford. I really can't remember a time when we did not know him. When I was in high school, he and John Bell would stop by the store (Taylor's Self-Service in Pilot Mountain, a family grocery store) on recruiting trips, just to make sure we were all staying in the fold. And even though I, like most younger brothers, was reluctant to follow my sister and brother, it became a fete accompli once Charlie had me come visit with Bruce Stewart concerning the Guilford Fellows program.

My closer association with Charlie actually started when we moved back to Greensboro in 1987. One day I got one of those 'let's have lunch' calls from him and it turned out that he wanted me to assist with the Guilford County regional group of the Alumni Association. That began many years of service that, among other benefits, has allowed me to connect with generations of fellow Guilfordians.

I do recall when Charlie was visiting for a family dinner once. Our grandfather was there and, never one to be indirect, he asked, 'Charlie, why did you never get married?' Charlie immediately answered, 'Never had time to court!' Guess he never did, as he was married to Guilford College. Of course, many of us do remember the large doll—that he called his wife— that sat in a rocker for several years in the front hall of Charlie's house."

GATHERING OF FRIENDS

Charlie's Christmas breakfasts, which occur all morning each Christmas Day, are legendary for both the quality and quantity of both food and guests. He only asks his guests to follow two rules—they have to arrive after eight o'clock and must leave before noon, and they must remember that once they're invited, they're always invited. To those who know Charlie, the second part of those instructions mirrors his friendship...once a friend, always a friend.

Amazingly, though he's cultivated thousands of friendships through his work, Charlie also doesn't believe that he's "done that much." "But," he professes, "there hasn't been a single day I haven't wanted to go to work. I've worked at Guilford every day except for one semester, the fall of 1983. I've never had a job interview and never had a resume. And I've never missed commencement. If I had it all to do over again, I wouldn't change a thing." So when was Charlie was at his peak? Was it in 1963, when he was put in charge of English Hall and helped to further mold students he had admitted himself only a year or two before? Was it in 1973, when he was hoisted onto the shoulders of future professional basketball players so that he could cut down a piece of Guilford College history? Was it in 1983, when he officially retired from the college, only to return to work less than a year later having had a building on campus named in his honor? Was it in 1993 when he celebrated his birthday at his home with over four hundred of his friends? Or is it in 2003, as he continues to impact a new generation of students?

It is all of these landmark years and the ones in between, for as former Guilford president Don McNemar has stated, "Charlie Hendricks has dedicated his life to Guilford College. The college and generations of young people are better for the caring concern and the personal support that Charlie has given to Guilford students over the decades."* Certainly those that have felt that concern and support over the years have been the students who might have been unable to attend Guilford were it not for Charlie enabling them to have a place to live for at least a portion of their college life.

It is no understatement, then, when Gary Thompson, class of 1968 and who was one of Charlie's boarders, says "Charlie Hendricks has been a constant beacon for Guilford College. I believe Charlie's greatest legacy will be that in his lifetime, he positively influenced more Guilford students than anyone else in the history of the school. Through the years, Charlie unselfishly has shared himself with others, opening his home to students in financial need and providing a warm place for friends to gather. As Director of Admissions, he had the ability to use intellectual and intuitive skills in making decisions about applicants, and many are the success stories resulting from his wisdom. As one who has been on staff in a variety of positions, Charlie continually provides an invaluable wealth of knowledge about Guilford alumni. Gary's wife Gail echoes those sentiments, exclaiming, "I have always loved Charlie Hendricks. He is one of those rare, ageless people who easily finds a special place in the hearts of friends of all ages. His charm, in part, is his love of life and his ability to enjoy the moment at hand. I am reminded of a 1992 gathering of Guilford friends in Duck, North Carolina. While sitting for hours on the beach, observing the ocean, Charlie commented that he could sit there all day because 'there is so much to see.' Thank you, Charlie, for helping us understand that life gives us many wonderful things to enjoy, if only we will open our eyes!"

In May of 1993, as Charlie turned seventy-five, hundreds of friends arrived and surrounded his yard to celebrate his birthday. More than a regular celebration, the day also served as a salute to a life dedicated to serving others. A group of several alumni, known as "The Washington Bunch," had formed a year earlier to plan the party and raise money for a scholarship to be named in Charlie's honor (which would first be awarded in 1997 to Guilford senior Santes Beatty). As Charlie McCurry, the admissions counselor who had stayed at Charlie's for five years, says, "I remember gathering for Charlie's birthday vividly. There was a tent in the yard, and people everywhere. Dignitaries abounded… Charlie Gaddy, the TV celebrity, Howard Coble, our representative in the House in DC, Dave Odom, then-Wake Forest basketball coach, and a host of other friends. My wife and I brought our five children with us. We were in the front yard when Charlie came out the front door and proceeded to trip over something and fall flat on the stage that had been set up on his porch. I thought, 'oh no, he's going to break his hip or back!' But typical Charlie, he got up laughing. The group there went on to give him some 'mad money' (which he probably ended up giving to some else), set up a scholarship for him at Guilford, and heaped accolades upon him about his life of generosity."

"Throughout his career at Guilford, Charlie has shown an irrepressible love of students and alums," Bill Rogers says simply. "Whether it was working in the soda shop, going to athletic events, guiding folks through the cafeteria, organizing hundreds of alumni gatherings, or just talking animatedly with old friends and newcomers alike throughout the campus—Charlie *enjoyed* students. Of course, there were always a few things that they did which Charlie disapproved of—and he would not hesitate to chide them. Through it all he was loyal and caring, and many became his lifelong friend. He went so far as to lend his car to students for dates, offer them many meals, and have a number of them live in the spare room of his outback 'red house.' What a giving guy!

It is really Charlie's great love and loyalty to his friends at Guilford that makes him so special. He shares so generously of himself that it is hard to express our thanks deeply enough. We are pleased to have had Charlie as part of our family gatherings for a number of years at Thanksgiving as well as at other times. We give profound thanks for the way he has been part of our lives, as well as so central to our beloved college."

A life of generosity. For Charlie Hendricks, a lifetime of giving of himself—to friends, family, and students—has provided him with rich rewards. His seventy-fifth birthday celebration provided him with a chance to address at least a portion of those who had felt his impact. A transcript of Charlie's thoughts to those assembled that day:

I feel like the little boy who fell into the molasses barrel... he said, "O, Lord, make my tongue worthy to the occasion.

This is a great honor—an honor I appreciate very much. Ten years ago I had a building named for me, and today a scholarship in my name is just great. The important thing is that it happened today while I am still living to enjoy it. I am not sure, but I think there are only two others that have this honor and they were two former presidents. This is doubly important for they were at the top of the list and I am near the bottom. I have not and will not catch Curt Hege. He has two buildings plus a professorship named after him.

There are so many people to thank and for fear I am going to leave someone out I am going to do it anyway. First of all the Washington Group—Bill Burchette, Danny McQueen, Henry McKay, Dick Rankin, and Gary Thompson, along with ten others. They had the idea, but knew they needed help, and called on Clarajo and Bill Pleasants, my good and closest friends. They added Bill and Bev Rogers and Gordon Soenksen. They in turn called on the entire development staff. To the Committee of Seventy-Five, I need to say 'thank you very much.' But equally, if not more important, are all of you that are here today. A great appreciation, and thank you very much, for being here and being a part of my seventy-fifth birthday.

Since this had been planned, I kept asking myself, 'why this honor?'

Was it because I loaned many of you my car, truck, or van? This started back in 1947 when Jean Ralls, Barney Baker, Peggy Cochrane, and Betty Cramer used my 1936 Chevy to travel to schools when they were doing their student-teaching... as well as driving many other places.

Is it because I let at least thirty of you live in my home (with little or no pay)?

Could it be that I have been in thirty-five of your weddings?

Could it be that I looked at your admission material with great care before making a decision?

Maybe it is because I was head resident of English Hall for several years and had the following men live there—Tom English, Andy Brown, Jimmie Bales, Jack Holley, Dick Rankin, Ray Durham, Tommy Barnes, Bookie Binkley, Carl Shoaf, Ron Davis, not to mention Henry McKay, Danny McQueen, Don Ford, Phil Ford, Dan Kuzma, Dave Odom, Fred Rabb, Jon Cox, Alan Miller, Billy Ragsdale, and Bob Bregard—he was a piece of work.

There are others, but you see what I am talking about—whatever the reason, I am very, very happy.

This is enough—I might get a big head if there is anything else done... a building ten years ago and now a scholarship. If any of you are thinking about changing Guilford's name to Hendricks University, get it out of your mind, for I will not let that happen.

I do want to invite you back twenty-five years from now for my 100th birthday. I will be here and want all of you to come back then. Again, thank you all for everything. Don't leave just because it says on the invitation five o'clock. I will be here, so stay as long as you can. I want to close with this:

May you, as my friends, live a long life. And may I live one day less, for what is life without friends. Ask Charlie.

ACKNOWLEDGMENTS

This project would not have been possible without contributions from the following:

William Abernethy, Rosalie Adams, Clay Alexander, Helen Allen, Herb Appenzeller, Dick Baddour, Barb Bausch, Kenny Browning, Kent Chabotar, Joyce Clark, Howard Coble, Ruth Cross, Esther Cummings, Ralph Cummings, George Dixon, Randy Doss, Sheila Kendall Dunning, Marianna Edgerton, Anne Taylor Frost, Craig Fulton, Groome Fulton Jr., Phillip Fulton, Charles Gaddy, Dennis Haglan, Evelyn Harris, Don Howie, Jack Jensen, Mary Josey, Jeff Kloss, Sara Bohn Looman, Seth Macon, Jim Malone, Susan Manz, Monty Milner, Robert McLendon, Charlie McCurry, Brad McIlwaine, Henry McKay, Jennie Montgomery, Bob Newton, David Odom, Mark Owczarski, Charlie Patterson, Bill Pleasants, Jim Pleasants, Emily Pryor, Bob Ralls, Jace Ralls, Jean Ralls, Peter Reichard, Beverly Rogers, William Rogers, David Stanfield, Bill Starling, Bruce Stewart, Thomas Taylor, Steve Taylor, Lloyd Taylor, Gail Thompson, Gary Thompson, Cornelia Warlick, Bill Wearmouth, Winslow Womack, and Bill Yates.

Special thanks to:

Deidre Albert, Wendy Davis, Jerry Harrelson, Clarajo Pleasants, Libby Rich, Katie Severa, Misty Thebeau, Edwina Woodbury, and the Guilford College Office of Alumni Relations.

Cover Photo by:
Susan Mullally Clark of Greensboro, North Carolina.

Community Newsletter, Guilford College, Vol 12, No.13, January 15, 2002